"Would you like to understand [the] Son and Holy Ghost? This, and many other significant TRINITIES, is artfully examined in this book. You will be amazed, as was I, to learn that we are literally immersed in a sea of trinities. But there is a surprise in store for the reader! The first eight chapters of this book will provide answers to your questions; in the remainder of the book, you will learn to believe; finish the book, and you are prepared to receive. Indeed, a key trinity is: ask, believe, and receive. Marie Jones and Larry Flaxman explain the technique in detail. I highly recommend this book. It will show you the way."

—Dr. John L. Turner, author of *Medicine, Miracles and Manifestations*

"Are we all living trinities? The Trinity Secret is E-ride that starts with 'The Holy Trinity,' winds through a 'Ladder of Consciousness,' 'Cosmic Memory Banks,' and the 'Grail Legends,' to conclude with the disclosure of a deep secret."

—Dick Sutphen, author of *Soul Agreements*

"As we transform into the evolutionary age of Aquarius, we move past the need for gurus and masters to create our spiritual path. Secret teachings once taught in ancient temples, are now being brought forward into the light for all those who have the eyes in which to see them. In The Trinity Secret Jones and Flaxman, reveal these age old principles which have been revered by wisdom cultures from around the world. In sharing this knowledge, they offer a sacred gift, uniting the divine masculine and the divine feminine energy with the higher self and remind us, that the power of three will truly set us free!"

—Kala Ambrose, author of *9 Life Altering Lessons* and host of *The Explore Your Spirit with Kala Show*

"The Trinity Secret is a fascinating book about the most powerful symbol of life; the trinity is a symbol of creativity, stability, and unity. It is the symbol designed to attract high-dimensional energy and enhance perfection. This book reveals the true secret behind the power of three, which we all should know. I highly recommend reading this book for your own spiritual evolution."

—Dr. Carmen Harra, author of *The Eleven Eternal Principles*

The Trinity Secret

The Power of Three
and the Code of Creation

Marie D. Jones
and
Larry Flaxman

New Page Books
A Division of The Career Press, Inc.
Franklin Lakes, N.J.

THE TRINITY SECRET
EDITED BY JODI BRANDON
TYPESET BY GINA HOOGERHYDE
Cover design by Ian Shimkoviak/the Book Designers

Images on pages 22, and 138 courtesy of Wikimedia.
Images on pages 33, 52, 118, 119, and 158 courtesy of Wikipedia.
Images on pages 86, 93, 98, 109, and 149 courtesy of Wikimedia Commons.
Image on page 141 courtesy of Istock.

Images on pages 85 are in the public domain and available from various outlets.

Printed in the U.S.A.

To order this title, please call toll-free 1-800-CAREER-1 (NJ and Canada: 201-848-0310) to order using VISA or MasterCard, or for further information on books from Career Press.

The Career Press, Inc.
220 West Parkway, Unit 12
Pompton Plains, NJ 07444
www.careerpress.com
www.newpagebooks.com

Library of Congress Cataloging-in-Publication Data

CIP information available upon request.

Dedication

For Max and Mary Essa.

Acknowledgments

Marie and Larry would like to thank Michael Pye, Laurie Kelly-Pye, and the entire staff at New Page Books—your belief in us, and in our work is what keeps us going. We are so grateful that you allow us to write the kinds of books we love to write and get the ideas out there as a part of the bigger dialogue. Thanks also to the wonderful staff at Warwick Associates, for their fantastic publicity and promotion of our books. Thanks to Suzanne Weaver for the fantastic Website work. You make us look good!

Marie would like to thank:

My mom, Milly, and my dad, John, for ongoing support, inspiration, and love and for keeping me "me." Thanks to my best friend, my sister, Angella, and my kid brother, John, who makes me laugh out loud, and to my extended family, Winnie, Alana, Aaron, Ally, Ef, and to all my dear friends old and new who continue to support and put up with me. Onward and upward, Helen! Thanks to everyone who listens to me on the radio, comes to see me speak, and buys and actually reads my books! Yeah, I know some of you just use them as doorstops. It's okay.

Thanks to Lisa Hagan for being my champion, and to Bruce Lucas for allowing me to take it to a whole new level. Thanks to Wendy Kram, too, for believing in me, and my ideas. It still amazes me the fantastic people that my work has drawn into my life!!! I love it when I get an e-mail from someone who says they read my book and like my work. The feeling never gets old. I always wanted to make a difference.

Thanks most of all to the funniest, cutest, most amazing human being that ever walked the earth: my kid, Max. I can't even put into words what I feel when you tell me to "get a life" or when I watch you sleeping. Your wise-beyond-your-years sense of humor, your cutting sarcasm, your ability to fix any computer problem known to humankind. You are the smartest kid I've ever known. And the biggest smart-ass. As you grow up, you just keep getting cooler, funnier and cuter. You're my sidekick and my pal, always.

Lucy, thanks for tearing apart my expensive sectional.

And of course, I have to thank Larry Flaxman, who came into my life just three short years ago, and changed it forever. Four books and counting. Hundreds of shows, articles, events. And I am still just as excited, if not more so, to see where this all leads us. It's been a non-stop ride, chaotic at times, but worth every twist and turn. The work we are doing together is amazing even to me. I have to pinch myself to remind me that it is real, and I sense we have even bigger things in store. From what I hear out there in the world, we make one hell of a team! But then we always knew that, didn't we?

Larry would like to thank:

Wow, where to start? I am grateful for so much in my life that an entire book could be written of my acknowledgments alone! I would certainly be remiss if I didn't mention my mom, Sheila, my dad, Norman, and my brother, Jon, for their constant encouragement, support, and motivation in everything I do. It truly is wonderful having such a close-knit and connected family. Secondly, I would like to thank my dear wife, Emily, who truly must have the heart of an angel…especially with her never-ending patience and ability to put up with me! Whether I'm working, traveling, speaking, or writing she has endured my often-scarce presence with few objections. Many thanks to those I've befriended as a result of my research, books, speaking engagements, radio shows, and TV appearances. I can't even being to thank all of my fans enough for your support and encouragement. Please know that you guys and gals are the best! It is truly humbling to know that so many people are behind me!

A special thank you to my partner and dear friend, Marie D. Jones. It certainly doesn't seem like three years! I would never have imagined that after reading *PSIence*, and sending my heartfelt thanks for bringing exposure to a topic that I felt was sorely lacking in the paranormal field, that we would be where we are now! Four books, more radio shows than I can possibly remember, magazine articles, TV appearances, and movies! What next? I can certainly say that whatever we do is going to be big!

Lastly, and certainly most importantly I wish to thank my "little buddy": Mary Essa. You are the most amazing, beautiful, and intelligent daughter ever. You manage to make all that is wrong in the world right. Your boundless energy, smile, and curiosity drive, inspire, and move me beyond words. After a hard day, I can always count on you to greet me at the door with your arms outspread and your angelic voice saying "I missed you, Daddy." Until you came into my life, I had no idea how deep love truly can be. I do now. Euripides said it best: "To a father growing old nothing is dearer than a daughter."

"I am not afraid of tomorrow, for I have seen yesterday and I love today."
—William Allen White

Contents

Authors' Note

When it comes to the number 3, things can get quite confusing. Throughout this book you will see references to trinities, triads, tripartite and triune, triplicate, triangle, and, well, even thrice. A basic rundown of terms will hopefully help keep things in order, but remember: It all means "associated with 3!"

TRIAD: forming a group of three, such as three entities, three Gods or Goddesses, three little pigs. Triads usually appear together and are inter-related.

TRIUNE: having the nature of three-in-one, or one-in-three. Something with three manifestations or essences, but all one being.

TRIPARTITE: triple parts, as in three heads of a beast, or three arms.

TRIANGLE: the three-sided shape we all know and love.

TRIPLICATE: something that is duplicated three times.

TRINITY: similar to triune, three-in-one—three parts of a unified whole.

THRICE: three times in power, volume, and measurement.

We hope that this makes it a little less confusing, and apologize in advance for using one to describe the other. Oftentimes the terms are interchangeable, or exist in conjunction with each other. For example, a triad of Gods can also have a unifying Trinitarian aspect and a triune nature as well. And the triune nature of something might also make it a trinity but not a triplicate or triad. Other sources might refer to, say, the Classical Greek deities of Zeus, Leto, and Apollo as a triad, whereas some might call them triple deities. Others might look at Upper, Lower, and Middle as the triune nature of a Shaman's reality, yet others will say it is a triple world. People might call themselves "thrice great," or just triple awesome. Honestly, it all pretty much means the same thing: that the number 3 is involved.

Introduction:
In the Beginning

We have all likely heard the popular saying "Behind every great man stands a great woman," but how many of us are aware that behind every great religious system stands a great metaphysical concept? And what if many hidden teachings or powerful truths end up buried by the authoritarian orthodoxy and condemned as heresy? Taking this one step further, what if behind every metaphysical concept is a scientific theory that serves as the bedrock and foundation of that greater truth?

As authors, our journey began a scant two years ago. The discovery of "The Trinity Secret" began when we wrote our first book together, *11:11—The Time Prompt Phenomenon: The Meaning Behind Mysterious Signs, Sequences, and Synchronicities*. In that book, we explored in depth the profound nature of numbers, mathematics, and the almost magical role of mathematical theory in the creation and structure of the cosmos—and even of life itself. Interestingly, of all the numbers that we researched, the number 3 seemed to come up most frequently, and as we would later uncover, usually as a sacred and profane number with a common denominator.

In books about Buddhism we found it. In books about the levels of consciousness and Jungian analysis we found it. In books about Wicca and shamanism and earth religions we found it. We found it in the Kabbalah, the Bhagavad-Gita, and the Tao Te Ching. We found it in Science of Mind textbooks and Unity prayer guides. It was even found in such esoterica as the mystery schools of Freemasonry and the Rosicrucian Order. We found it in *The Secret*. We found it in numer-ology, and we even found it in books about cutting-edge discoveries in quantum physics, Noetics, and unified field theory! In short, we found it everywhere! Was this simply coincidence…or providence?

The concept we are referring to is the Holy Trinity—the triune nature of the creative force and our interaction with it. This idea of a triadic basis for a creative force (many call it God) presented itself over and over, in different forms, symbology, and semantics. Incredible as it may seem, we found something even more stunning and exciting. Something that at first might appear to be anti-religion—or even profane: The Holy Trinity was not what many of us been taught it was in grade-school catechism classes.

In fact, everything led us to believe that the Trinity was not what the churches said it was at all. Instead, we found interesting clues to a powerful core concept in this Holy Trinity that was not indigenous to any one religion, but to all religions (even though most Roman Catholic clergy would never admit this common bond!). What was once only this vague idea of "the Father, the Son, and the Holy Spirit" and encompassing three separate entities suddenly became something far grander. Suddenly this concept became more experiential and spiritual than physical and visible. The three "people" that we had once been taught about no longer made sense as "people," but only began to make sense when presented in more metaphysical terms. We viewed these archetypes as symbols of a much deeper process before it began to make sense. This is a process that took place within us—internally, and not somewhere above us or far beyond our grasp. Yet, it was also an integral part of the world of cutting-edge science and quantum theory.

So often had we all heard that the Father was God, the Son was Jesus, and the Holy Ghost was some spectral presence that would choose to "descend" upon a chosen person, filling that person with the Glory of God. That was that, no questions asked. Three separate people, three individual entities, and none of them personal or accessible to a normal person unless you followed strict church doctrine and lived a life without sin (and then, of course, you still ran the risk of not warranting a visit from the Holy Ghost, as if some kind of divine lottery was at work).

But the more we realized that this idea of three outside entities imparting divine union made no sense spiritually, intuitively, or intellectually, the more the truth became obvious, yet hidden in plain sight to most. The Trinity had to mean more. It had to have a deeper explanation—a more symbolic interpretation. And to think it could only serve the orthodox Christian population? Well, that would mean that the secrets of creation were available only to a select chosen few. Arrogant and extremely narrow-minded indeed.

As the mystery of the Trinity began to unfold for us, we realized that it was present in all religions, but that not all religions or spiritual systems chose to refer to it as the Holy Trinity. Sometimes, we had to dig deep into a spiritual system's history and beliefs to find it, yet other times it was right there, visibly present under a different nomenclature, but easily identifiable as a Trinity that led to different states of awareness and being associated with Divine union. That is when we began to understand on an experiential level, rather than just an intellectual level, that the concept of Trinity was actually much bigger than a biblical reference or simply a way to finish off a prayer. This Trinity was a cornerstone, a foundation block, a code, a blueprint, and *a secret!* Like a source of water that feeds a million rivers, the concept of the Trinity is a source that feeds a bounty of religions with water that is sweet, pure, and nourishing to all who drink of it.

That the Trinity serves as a basis for all the great spiritual and philosophical systems, including the oldest of those systems, really

In the Beginning

should come as no surprise to those who have studied metaphysics. Long before the Old and New Testaments were written, this concept of a triadic nature of Divine Union reared its head again and again. From the creation tales of the ancient civilizations to the mythologies of the Greek, Norse, Romans, and Celts, the model of a triadic divinity is pervasive. The concepts of human, superhuman, and divine speak of the triadic nature of Oneness. So, too, do the states of consciousness of the mind, from the id to the ego to the superego. This triadic nature appears as the popular concepts of Principal, Universal, and Material, and of Conscious, Subconscious, and Physical.

Followers of Truth know that truth is unchanging, but often shows itself in a variety of masks and faces, symbols and riddles. We were quick to learn that the Trinity was no different, leading us to believe it to be an archetype—a symbol present in the collective unconscious of humankind from the beginning of time. The more we studied the common links between spirituality and science, the more that we realized that this symbol had at its very foundation a metaphysical, rather than religious or doctrinal, basis. In other words, the Trinity was not just something we could read about, study, and understand only if we were confirmed Catholics or Christians, but an *actual process* that we could engage in and experience whether we were Wiccan, Hindu, Atheist, or Buddhist. A process, our research would prove, that could lead us directly to the field of pure potentiality—the Grid of reality, so to speak—and the secret of creation itself.

Most exciting of all was our research into quantum physics, where new discoveries in string theory, multiple universes, perception, human consciousness, and the Zero Point Field gave us even more proof that a triune nature of creation existed all around us, and that we, without aid of priests, bishops, or popes, could become co-creators ourselves, linking up with the One True Source by way of this secret teaching. Gnostics knew this, as did Hermes the Great, who taught that "As Above, So Below." Physicist David Bohm refers to the triune nature of reality as having three distinct orders: the explicate, or manifest reality; the implicate, invisible grid of connectivity; and the superimplicate, almost Godlike order. He, too, knew the secret.

The Trinity Secret

The problem with metaphysical concepts serving as the basis for organized religious doctrine is that many, if not all, organized religions are led by people with powerful motivations and incentives to claim truths as exclusively their own. Admit that their teachings are based on metaphysical truths? Hah! Agree that their precious Trinity can be found in other forms in other traditions? No way! Most major religions would sooner engage in an all-out holy war than admit to this blasphemy! Think of the ramifications! Could we be right in assuming that this idea of Trinity, of "the Father and the Son and the Holy Spirit" as being a sort of "recipe" for union with the creative force was something that could eventually be embraced as common ground among all religions? Most organized religions struggle so hard to maintain their distinct "organization," rather than focusing on how they can all best work together for the common good. Could this research even begin to give credence to a basic foundation from which sprung all other religious thought and doctrine in a world of ignorant clergy and their equally ignorant followers determined to kill each other over who is right and who is wrong?

What if they were *all* right?

Still, the questions persist. If the Holy Trinity is such a common concept, then why haven't more people caught on? And if it is such a simple process toward enlightenment, then why haven't more people become enlightened? These are questions we will explore further in *The Trinity Secret*. Perhaps we will answer them; perhaps they will never be answered. The amount of light shed on dark places often depends on the ability to get one's work and ideas out into the world, where others can read it and respond to it from their own experience.

Often, what appears to be easy is terribly hard. On the contrary, the most difficult concepts to grasp intellectually are often the most simple in nature to understand and embrace intuitively. And often the best place to hide something is in plain sight, where few people ever think to look for it. We have a feeling the Trinity Secret is one of these frustrating paradoxes. But it is not an impossible paradox, not by far.

All of us are on wonderfully diverse and excitingly unique paths leading toward the same awesome ultimate Truth. The truth is that we are all connected on a deeper, unseen level, like a World Wide Web—

In the Beginning

an invisible order of Oneness. A true "unified field." In a world like that, war and greed would vanish. In a world like that, religion would become a source of joy, not of bloodshed and intolerant ignorance, violence, and vehemence. In a world like that, human potential and individual expression would soar on wings of eagles.

We would like to see that world. Perhaps *The Trinity Secret* will help reveal this truth, and the power we all have access to that will bring us into direct knowing of what we really are: *creators!*

1

Three Into One: A (Very) Brief History of the Trinity

In the name of the Father, the Son, and the Holy Spirit....

For hundreds of years, millions of people have begun their morning or evening prayers with the words *In the name of the Father, the Son, and the Holy Spirit*. Yet few truly comprehend the nature of a triune God that is also the One God. Though our intention for this book certainly does not focus solely on the concept of Christian Trinity, we would be remiss as authors not to present the history behind the development of the Trinitarian doctrine of the world's largest religion.

As you may likely be aware, the Holy Trinity is a central mystery to those who call themselves Christians. Yet it contains the seeds of what we will be discussing in future chapters. Three into one as a process or description of divine energy, the universal power of the number 3, the triune nature of reality and creation itself—these are but a few of the things that we will explore on our journey into this mysterious concept.

For those who grew up celebrating the Trinity as a part of their religious tradition, the idea of three Gods as one God, or three parts of God as the whole of God, still boggles the mind and seems to cause much debate and conflict among theologians and historians alike. Does anyone really know what the Trinity means? Or is it truly an abstract idea meant to be embraced by the heart with only faith as evidence of its meaning? Does the Trinity have a special meaning to you?

We authors state that the following is but a brief summary of the history of the Trinity in Christian theology (see the Bibliography for books that go in-depth on this), as this is not the crux of the book's implications. However, it is important to know how the most widely known Trinitarian concept got to be such a big, if not enigmatic, part of the doctrine, and to see where the seeds of a wider understanding of the Trinity were planted in the soil of modern belief.

In Mark 12:29 of the New Testament, Jesus is quoted as saying "The Lord our God is One." So where, then, did this idea of three entities come from?

Fig. 1-1

The shield of the Trinity is also known as *Scutum Fideli* (Latin for "shield of the faith") and is a Christian symbol that expresses the Trinity doctrine. It was not intended as an actual "blueprint" or diagram of God, but rather a visual interpretation of the triune nature of God, sometimes as a triangle with point up; sometimes inverted. It was especially revered in medieval France and England as an emblem of God, and is found in many manuscripts and texts of that time period. The actual origins of the symbols are not known, although scholars suggest may come from as early as the 12th century. The nodes and connecting links suggest that the center, which is God, is and is not the Father and Son and Holy Spirit. Although this certainly is confusing to say the least, the paradox of Christian Trinity doctrine that holds to this day is one of the greatest religious mysteries. It is also referred to as the "Arms of the Faith," "Emblem of the Trinity," and "Shield of the Blessed Trinity."

Throughout the Old Testament of the Bible, God is referred to as the Father, the One God, and the *only One God*. But nowhere is the word *trinity* to be found, let alone a concept of a triune God. The word *trinity* itself comes from the Latin *trinitas*, which means "triad" or "the number three," and has a Greek corresponding word that first appeared in Christian theology around AD 170. Theophilus of Antioch, who became Patriarch or Bishop of Antioch in AD 168, spoke of a trinity, although not within the context of Christian belief. He instead attributed it to God, His Word (Logos), and His Wisdom (Sophia), and his trinity may have been a comment on the Book of Genesis and the first act of creation. Theophilus suggested that Sun was the image of God (he was born a pagan, so still had his pagan Sun God concepts to wrangle with!) and the moon as Man, or the Son, because the moon represented a death and resurrection based upon its natural phases.

In the New Testament, there are mentions of the Father, the Son, and the Holy Spirit. Such significant revelations as Matthew's Great Commission to "Go therefore and make disciples of all nations, baptizing them in the name of the Father and of the Son and of the Holy Spirit" (Matt 28:19) and later Paul's "The grace of the Lord Jesus Christ and the love of God and the fellowship of the Holy Spirit be with you all"

Three Into One

(2 Cor: 13–14). Never, though, was the Trinity directly referred to. Likewise, no doctrine was ever mentioned as part of the belief in the teachings imparted by Christ. That came later, mainly in the time of Greek Apologists during AD 130–180, when for some reason humankind's understanding of the nature of God's Oneness began morphing into a Trinitarian view. It may have had something to do with the teaching of pre-Christian Greek philosophers trying to understand the nature of this "Logos," as found in John 1:1.

Logos would come to be associated with Christ, the Word of God made flesh, and would pose the question: Are God and Christ the same, two different people, or what? The Oneness of God itself was being challenged by the suggestion that this Logos or Christ was also divine, although subservient to the Father, God. Still, this would ultimately imply two divine entities, not one.

It wasn't until the third century that Latin theologian Tertullian referred to the Trinity of Father, Son, and Holy Spirit as one essence—however, not one person. He himself was not a Trinitarian, but rather believed that the Holy Ghost was not God or even a person, but more of a "thing" or substance. Tertullian later adopted the idea of a divine nature and eternal personhood of the Holy Spirit as well, thus launching what most scholars believe was the birth of the Trinitarian belief we know today, with God as three "persons" but one essence, one God. Tertullian's model of God was made up of one "substantia" or substance, and three separate personas, or distinct persons, created to defend Christian monotheism in the face of the threat from Gnostic polytheism. In other words, the three distinct persons were a part of the substance of the One God. But Tertullian's concept of "person" was different than ours. It is important to understand that in his concept, he was not implying three people each with their own consciousness and individuality, or that the Son is a lesser deity than the Father.

Origen, a theologian and Christian scholar living between AD 185 and AD 254, would add his own spin, based in part of pagan Greek beliefs, that Jesus was the first born of the Father, but that the Holy Spirit was associated in honor and dignity with the Father and Son. But, writing in his book *On the Principles*, he went on to state that it is not clear whether the Holy Spirit was "to be regarded as born or innate, or also as a Son of God or not." He did teach that the three persons of the Trinity were eternal, although not necessarily equal. Still, the word *trinity* was never mentioned, even though more thinkers and theologians writing in this time period were coming around to the Trinitarian way of thought.

In AD 260, Sabellius, a priest and theologian, was actually excommunicated and labeled a heretic for stating that there was only one "person" in the Godhead, and that the Father, Son, and Holy Spirit were the same person, sharing one divinity and one alone. This Godhead could manifest in many different ways, as Father, as Son, as Holy Spirit, but ultimately was one "person."

Sabellius's critics attacked his concept, with one, Gregory the Wonder Worker, actually commenting in a volume of *A Sectional Confession of Faith* in AD 260 that "There are indeed three persons, inasmuch as there is one person of God the Father, and one of the Lord the Son, and one of the Holy Spirit; and yet that there is but one divinity, inasmuch as... there is one substance of the trinity." Even the Council of Rome spoke out against Sabellius, stating in the *Tome of Damasus* (canon 2) that those who follow Sabellius's teaching would be "anathematized."

As early as the first century AD, Bishop Clement repeatedly referenced the Father, Son, and Holy Spirit in his writings. This was long before the actual development of Trinity doctrine in the fourth century; however, it shows that the necessity of a Trinitarian concept existed. Perhaps it was a way to coalesce ideas from the Hebrew scriptures into an understandable nature of God and God's works through the church. The same references can be found in the writings of Ignatius, Bishop of Antioch, who wrote letters before his execution in Rome that speak of the Father, "Jesus Christ our God," and the Holy Spirit. Ignatius also referred to Christ as "the mind of the Father."

The Trinity Emerges

Early hints of God, the Son, and the Holy Spirit were evident in the catechetical document "The Didache," in a baptismal formula that is Trinitarian; again the Father, Son, and Holy Spirit. In *The Martyrdom of Polycarp*, we find Bishop Polycarp confessing to the "Lord God Almighty,

Father of your beloved son Jesus Christ," and later asking to be received among the number of martyrs "in the incorruptibility of the Holy Spirit."

Other early mentions appear in second-century AD writings, such as *The Epistle of Barnabas*, describing Christ as pre-existent, and the Son as Lord of the whole world. God's purpose was to be fulfilled through Christ in the world. Later in the epistle there is a reference to the Holy Spirit, but far less than those describing the relationship between God and the Son.

But it was at the First Council of Nicaea in AD 325 that the concept of the Trinity was to be forever forged into Christian belief and theology. It was at this Council that the Athanasian Creed was created, a creed which stated:

Whosoever will be saved, before all things it is necessary that he hold the Catholic Faith. Which Faith except every one do keep whole and undefiled; without doubt he shall perish everlastingly. And the Catholic Faith is this: That we worship one God in Trinity, and Trinity in Unity; Neither confounding the Persons; nor dividing the Essence. For there is one Person of the Father; another of the Son; and another of the Holy Ghost. But the Godhead of the Father, of the Son, and of the Holy Ghost, is all one; the Glory equal, the Majesty coeternal. Such as the Father is; such is the Son; and such is the Holy Ghost. The Father uncreated; the Son uncreated; and the Holy Ghost uncreated. The Father unlimited; the Son unlimited; and the Holy Ghost unlimited. The Father eternal; the Son eternal; and the Holy Ghost eternal. And yet they are not three eternals; but one eternal. As also there are not three uncreated; nor three infinites, but one uncreated; and one infinite. So likewise the Father is Almighty; the Son Almighty; and the Holy Ghost Almighty. And yet they are not three Almighties; but one Almighty. So the Father is God; the Son is God; and the Holy Ghost is God. And yet they are not three Gods; but one God. So likewise the Father is Lord; the Son Lord; and the Holy Ghost Lord. And yet not three Lords; but one Lord. For like as we are compelled by the Christian verity; to acknowledge every Person by himself to be God and Lord; So are we forbidden by the Catholic Religion; to say, There are three Gods, or three Lords. The Father is made of none; neither created,

The Trinity Secret

nor begotten. The Son is of the Father alone; not made, nor created; but begotten. The Holy Ghost is of the Father and of the Son; neither made, nor created, nor begotten; but proceeding. So there is one Father, not three Fathers; one Son, not three Sons; one Holy Ghost, not three Holy Ghosts. And in this Trinity none is before, or after another; none is greater, or less than another. But the whole three Persons are coeternal, and coequal. So that in all things, as aforesaid; the Unity in Trinity, and the Trinity in Unity, is to be worshipped. He therefore that will be saved, let him thus think of the Trinity.

Furthermore it is necessary to everlasting salvation; that he also believe faithfully the Incarnation of our Lord Jesus Christ. For the right Faith is, that we believe and confess; that our Lord Jesus Christ, the Son of God, is God and Man; God, of the Essence of the Father; begotten before the worlds; and Man, of the Essence of his Mother, born in the world. Perfect God; and perfect Man, of a reasonable soul and human flesh subsisting. Equal to the Father, as touching his Godhead; and inferior to the Father as touching his Manhood. Who although he is God and Man; yet he is not two, but one Christ. One; not by conversion of the Godhead into flesh; but by assumption of the Manhood into God. One altogether; not by confusion of Essence; but by unity of Person. For as the reasonable soul and flesh is one man; so God and Man is one Christ; Who suffered for our salvation; descended into hell; rose again the third day from the dead. He ascended into heaven, he sitteth on the right hand of the God the Father Almighty, from whence he will come to judge the quick and the dead. At whose coming all men will rise again with their bodies; And shall give account for their own works. And they that have done good shall go into life everlasting; and they that have done evil, into everlasting fire. This is the Catholic Faith; which except a man believe truly and firmly, he cannot be saved.

This is the first creed to explicitly state the equality of the three persons of the Trinity. It was adopted and has been used by Catholic churches since the sixth century AD. Interestingly, modern scholars question today whether Athanasius of Alexandria, the famous defender of Nicene theology, truly authored this creed while in exile in Rome.

Three Into One

His name, though, has now been attached to the creed as a symbol of Trinitarian belief.

Most Catholics are more familiar with the Apostles' Creed, which also mentions the Trinity:

1. I believe in God, the Father almighty, creator of heaven and earth.
2. I believe in Jesus Christ, his only Son, our Lord.
3. He was conceived by the power of the Holy Spirit and born of the Virgin Mary.
4. He suffered under Pontius Pilate, was crucified, died, and was buried.
5. He descended into hell. On the third day he rose again.
6. He ascended into heaven and is seated at the right hand of the Father.
7. He will come again to judge the living and the dead.
8. I believe in the Holy Spirit,
9. the holy catholic Church, the communion of saints,
10. the forgiveness of sins,
11. the resurrection of the body,
12. and life everlasting.

Allegedly, the 12 apostles came under the inspiration of the Holy Spirit after Pentecost, each then dictating one of its traditional 12 articles. Also known as "The Symbol of the Apostles," this widely known creed is also used in the Lutheran, Anglican, and Western Orthodox churches. It appears to date back to AD 390 and was first mentioned in a letter from the Council of Milan to Pope Siricius, which stated, "Let them give credit to the Creed of the Apostles...." In its full form, it is believed the actual creed first appeared in the "Excerpt from Individual Canonical Books" of St. Priminius between AD 701 and AD 714. Though there is no firm origin source, this may have been the first time the longer version of a collection of shorter beliefs found throughout the New Testament were congealed into a creed that first arose in France and Spain before being widely accepted in Rome.

Today, modern Roman Catholic and Lutheran churches use this creed for baptismal rites and as a profession of faith during Mass.

The Trinity Secret

Similar in nature is the Nicene Creed, named for the Latin *Symbolum Nicaenum*. Is the most widely used throughout Christian liturgy. The first ecumenical council of the city of Nicaea adopted the creed at the Council in AD 325, and it was later revised by the First Council of Constantinople in AD 381. The original creed affirmed Christ's divinity and referred to him as "God," and the later revised creed introduced the Holy Spirit, which was worshipped and glorified along with the Father and the Son. In the latter part of the sixth century AD Western European Latin churches to the procession of the Holy Spirit added the words *and the son*. These words were not included in the original Nicene Creed, or the latter version revised by Constantinople.

Although the Athanasian Creed would describe this Trinitarian relationship in far more detail, the Nicene Creed became the foundation, or accepted yardstick, of traditional Christian belief, although evangelicals and fundamentalists would later reject the creed not as having full authority due to the fact that it was not a part of the Bible itself.

The current Nicene Creed used most widely today is as follows.

> We believe in one God,
> the Father, the Almighty
> maker of heaven and earth,
> of all that *is seen* and unseen.
> We believe in one Lord, Jesus Christ,
> the only Son of God,
> eternally begotten of the Father,
> God from God, Light from Light,
> true God from true God,
> begotten, not made,
> *one in Being* with the Father.
> Through him all things were made.
> For us men and for our salvation
> he came down from heaven
> by the power of the Holy Spirit
> he *was born of* the Virgin Mary, and *became* man.
> For our sake he was crucified under Pontius Pilate;
> he *suffered, died*, and was buried.

Three Into One

On the third day he rose again
in *fulfillment of* the Scriptures;
he ascended into heaven
and is seated at the right hand of the Father.
He will come again in glory to judge the living and the dead,
and his kingdom will have no end.
We believe in the Holy Spirit, the Lord, the giver of Life,
who proceeds from the Father and the Son.
With the Father and the Son he is worshipped and glorified.
He has spoken through the Prophets.
We believe in one holy catholic and apostolic Church.
We acknowledge one baptism for the forgiveness of sins.
We look for the resurrection of the dead,
and the life of the world to come. Amen.

Even this version contains additional words and phrases that were put in place to avoid confusion between what was written and the spoken interpretation.

This is a brief history of the Trinity as we know today, and in no way contains the full scope of controversy and confusion that the concept of God as three persons (but one God) carried with it throughout the centuries. These creeds solidified the Trinity as a distinct and foundational part of Christian theology, even if no one still truly understands what the Trinity really meant. Saint Augustine once described the Trinity as three parts of an individual human being: mind, spirit, and will. Three aspects of humanness, yet all are part of one greater whole, and together make for a unified human being.

Rejection of the Trinity

Judaism and Islam, the other two great Western traditions, rejected the Trinity for different reasons. Judaism rejected the concept based upon the grounds of Jesus's divinity, which was believed to be blasphemous. Whereas Islam strongly denies the Trinity, it appears to recognize it as Father, Son, and Maryam or Mary. Mormons believe

The Trinity Secret

in a triune Godhead that is made up of three distinct entities that are one in purpose. Unitarians reject the Trinity, believing instead in the oneness of God. Jehovah's Witnesses believe that only the Father is the one true God, Jesus is his firstborn son, and the Holy Spirit is not a person at all, but the active force of God. Other denominations denying the Trinity include Oneness Pentecostals, Unification Church, and the Christadelphians. During the Protestant Reformation of the 1500s, non-Trinitarians were executed or had to practice their beliefs in secret. (Sir Isaac Newton was one such secret believer.)

Some of these concepts will be explored more fully in later chapters, for they contain the seeds of a more metaphysical approach to the idea of a Trinity. This approach is even mirrored in many other teachings as well as life itself. But first we must ask: Why take the one God of the Old Testament, the Father and Creator, and turn him into three parts, three persons?

Necessity. Obligation. Inevitability.

Swiss theologian Emil Brunner wrote in *The Christian Doctrine of God: Dogmatics, Volume 1* that the Trinity doctrine may have been a "defensive doctrine," because the doctrine itself is not mentioned directly in scripture. But the implications of this said that Trinity did exist, and the concept of Christ as the Son or Logos, and God the Father, along with the Holy Spirit's mission in the church, moved the Trinity doctrine to the forefront of Christian belief.

In *The Trinity: Guides to Theology*, Roger Olson and Christopher Hall state that the church fathers of the second through fourth centuries came to the realization of the Trinitarian doctrine after finding flaws with its opposite: "They found it necessary to invent terms such as *trinitas* (Trinity) and *homoousios* (of the same substance) to describe the relationship between the Father and his Son—the Logos (Word)—when confronted with heretics who denied the deity of Jesus Christ and the personhood of the Holy Spirit." Thus the Trinity developed amid debate and controversy, despite its creators insisting they were not "making up" the concept, but rather "simply exegeting divine revelation."

The belief in three separate Gods is called "tritheism." Perhaps the Trinity was a way for Christians to deny tritheism, yet still recognize the three personas of the One God. The Old Testament always referred to

God, or Yahweh, as "the one God." Establishing a firm doctrine, even if it was quite open to interpretation as to what exactly that doctrine meant, enabled Christians to reconcile the two concepts without resorting to blasphemy or heresy.

Rejecting the Trinity doctrine then would be akin to denying the Christian belief in God, Christ, and Holy Spirit, even if the actual relationship between the three were never intellectually understood. That God is considered One Being, with Three Personhoods (each with their own disparate mission and essential qualities), still causes confusion among those who wonder why God just can't be All One, or why settle at Three Personhoods, and not more.

Had Christ not received deity status at the Nicaean Council, perhaps the need for the Trinity might not have been so great. After all, if Jesus Christ was just a man, there would have been no need to align his role with that of God's, or the Holy Spirit's. However, this deity status demanded an explanation. Is God not Christ? Is Christ not God? Is Christ a human representative of God? After all, he was referred to as "Immanuel," which means "God with us." Who is what and what is whom? Are you confused yet?

Though the word *trinity* itself does not appear in the New Testament, the Matthew gospel features Jesus commanding his disciples to baptize people in the "name of the Father, the Son and the Holy Spirit." This is one of many references to the concept of One God, Three Personhoods found in the New Testament. The apostle John refers to Jesus as the Logos, or Word, of God. Part of God that entered the world in human form, but sparking another question: How can the Word of God be a person? A human?

In the Old Testament, the Word of God was an active, creative force. It's by the Word of God that all creation is born. "Let there be light," and so on. But the word *ruach* or *Spirit* is often used as well. The word is utilized more than 400 times as a "third way of articulating the creative, revelatory and redemptive activity of God," according to author Gerald O'Collins. In *The Tripersonal God: Understanding and Interpreting the Trinity*, he suggests that even the word *wisdom* or *sophia* was sometimes used to function synonymously with *word* and *spirit* calling the three terms "both identified with God and the divine activity and distinguished from God." These personified agents of divine activity were not to be interpreted as actual persons, even though they each possessed personal characteristics.

Fig. 1-2

Fig. 1-3

1-2: The Triquetra, or Trinity Knot, has become a popular symbol found on wedding and engagement rings, and was even used on the cover of the album Led Zeppelin 4, for those of you old enough to remember that band! 1-3: The shamrock, or three-leaf clover.

Two popular symbols used today have their roots in the Holy Trinity and the concept of three-into-one. The Triquetra, or Celtic Knot, is also called the Trinity knot and its three distinct sides are said to represent the Father, Son, and Holy Spirit. Mainly used during the 19th-century Celtic Revival, the Triquetra suggests the interconnected relationship of the three sides, all interlaced into one cohesive whole. The three sides are in the shape of the Vesica Piscis, another sacred symbol with two circles of equal radius intersecting so that the center of each lies on the circumference of the other. Today, the Triquetra are often used on wedding rings as the symbol of the divine union between two souls, uniting as one in holy matrimony. The symbol is also found in some newer revised Bibles on the title page, and is also considered sacred to Celtic witches and pagans as a symbol of life, death, and rebirth.

When the word Celtic is mentioned one might also think of leprechauns, rainbows, and shamrocks. Although some may believe that these symbols represent nothing more than fables or myth, were you aware that the Shamrock gets its mystical reputation from a legend? Long ago, during the times of the Druids, a bishop from Ireland by the name of Saint Patrick found one and picked it out of the ground, using it as an example of the trinity of the Father, Son, and Holy Spirit. To this day, shamrocks represent the spirit of Ireland, a predominately Catholic nation.

The Trinity doctrine would be altered, edited, changed, formed, and reformed throughout history in accordance with Church beliefs and needs of the times, although the crux would continue to be the doctrine established in and around the fourth century AD. But the fundamental concept would remain that the One God takes on three forms in order to accomplish the salvation and works of Christian belief. As the Father, God can create the world. As the Son, God can operate in the world of Man. As the Holy Spirit, God can impart grace, inspire good works, and further the mission of Christ's teachings.

Most of the noteworthy differences between the Trinity doctrines of the Catholics, Anglicans, Protestants, and Orthodox churches would focus on the Holy Spirit, the least-understood aspect of the triad, and its relationship with the Father and the Son. As we will see in future chapters, looking at the Trinity in a different light suggests that others had an understanding of the Spirit, the Breath of Life, as something other than a persona of the Divine.

Of the three personas, the Holy Spirit is the hardest concept to grasp. It is not a God, or a person like Christ representing God in human form on Earth. It is not even considered a "deity," but is considered divine, possibly grace or love or some gift from God. Yet, the Holy Spirit is often referred to throughout the New Testament, most notably by Paul in his Letters, as being "poured down upon" or "interceding" or "distributing" or "being filled with" as if it were both a person and a non-person. Certainly you cannot pour down a person upon another, but a person can distribute or intercede gifts of grace and forgiveness. God can give or send the Holy Spirit, and humans can receive the gift of the Spirit. The Son can also send the Spirit, as he does to the disciples in John's Gospel (16:7) after he is gone. This conflicting language adds to the mystique of the third "face" of the Trinity. Constantinople I affirmed the divinity of the Holy Spirit in the face of objections by the Macedonians, a sect named after a bishop who was condemned, and the Pneumatomachians, the Arians, and the Anomeans, all of whom denied the divine nature of the Holy Spirit. The Arians and the Anomeans also held Christ to an inferior status than God. The Trinity has always had its detractors, made even worse by the fact that even the believers couldn't quite fully come together on what the Trinity truly meant.

In the New Testament, in the Gospel of Luke, the Holy Spirit is mentioned as something that Jesus "rejoices in." Luke 10:21–22 begins with, "At that same hour, Jesus rejoiced in the Holy Spirit and said, 'Thank you, Father, Lord of heaven and earth, because you have hidden these things from the wise and intelligent and have revealed them to infants….'" This is mirrored in Matthew 11:25–27, and brings to light the whole Trinity in one passage, with Jesus addressing God as the Father, thus a distinction from himself. Jesus does not say, "I am the Father" but rather, "I thank you, Father." The Holy Spirit is also a distinct entity, one that Jesus rejoices in as he gives thanks to God.

Jesus held the role of the primary giver and sender of the Holy Spirit to others, along, of course, with God. With God, Jesus could pour the Spirit upon others, and the apostles or chosen ones could receive the Spirit. Paul differs in his Letters, though, suggesting instead that the Spirit may be simply "the Spirit of God" or "the Spirit of Christ." In *The Tripersonal God*, author Gerald O'Collins points out that based upon the interpretation of the word *of* we could read this to mean "the Spirit that brings us to God/Christ," "the Spirit that comes from or is drawn from God/Christ," *or* "the Spirit that IS God/Christ." If you recall in recent history, the word *of* created all kinds of interpretive drama for a former president! Here it can make all the difference between what the Holy Spirit is, at least in the eyes of Paul.

Interpreting the Trinity

Throughout the history of the Trinity in Christian theology, a true understanding has always been open to interpretation. Depending on the religious atmosphere of the times, elements were added, edited, or removed entirely from a more detailed doctrine, just as most scholars agree the Old and New Testaments were. To find an "original" Trinity document—one that fully and clearly states the exact meaning of the concept—would be impossible. But we sure do have a lot of interpretations!

A much more psychological approach was taken by the man considered to be one of the foremost figures in the development of Western Christianity, a man who was a great philosopher and theologian, and who would influence many great thinkers to come: Augustine of Hippo (AD 354–430). Augustine was also known as St. Augustine, St. Austin, and Bishop of Hippo. Historian Thomas Cahill referred to Augustine as the first medieval man and the last classical man. He spoke Latin and spent his earlier years immersed in the philosophies of Manicheism and the teachings of Plotinus.

In AD 387, he had a spiritual conversion and was baptized into Catholicism. St. Augustine became a key figure in the development of Trinitarian thought, as well as numerous other doctrines. In fact, there are more than 100 surviving works in print that ran the gamut from apologetic works against heretics, to texts examining Christian doctrine and commentary on the Bible. He is best known, though, for his *Confessiones* (*Confessions*), which documents his own personal life; *De civitate dei* (*City of God*), which was written to inspire confidence in Christians who were reeling from the sacking of Rome by the Visigoths; and *De trinitate* (*On the Trinity*), which introduced his own "psychological analogy" of the Trinity and is considered to be one of history's greatest theological works.

Augustine wrote *De trinitate* between AD 400 and AD 416. This was a critical piece that examined the reasoning behind the concept of three divine persons fitting into Christian monotheism. Augustine also delved into the triune God's meaning for humanity and how humanity in turn sees the triune God, constructing a written text that would become the foundation of how the Trinity was to be understood and interpreted throughout history to come. His main belief as stated in the text is the principle of inseparability: that the three "persons" of the Trinity must not be interchanged, but that they are inseparable as one, even if the work they do is of a separate nature. Thus, he states there is "the Father and the Son and the Holy Spirit—each one of these is God, and all of them together are God; each of these is a full substance and all together are one substance." They are three distinguishable persons, but with the same eternal nature, same majesty, and same power.

Augustine makes a nice distinction when he writes, "In the Father there is Unity," placing the Father, God, as the unifier. "And the three are all one because of the Father, all equal because of the Son, and all in harmony because of the Holy Spirit." He points to the human mind as a link to understanding the Father, Son, and Holy Spirit by his own construction of a trinity of memory, understanding, and will. In a rather complicated analogy, he makes his case: "Memory is the name of one only of those three, yet all the three concurred in producing the name of this single one of the three. The single word 'memory' could not be expressed but by the operation of the will, and the understanding, and the memory." He continues with the word *understanding*, which could not be expressed "but by the operation of the memory, the will and the understanding." The same goes for the will, the single word *will* unable to be expressed "but by the operation of the memory and the understanding and the will."

Ultimately, it is believed that Augustine was trying to say in *De trinitae* that "the Father, Son and Holy Spirit may be exhibited separately, by certain visible symbols, by certain forms borrowed from the creatures, and still their operations be inseparable." In the same fashion that memory, will, and understanding work, so does the Trinity, although Augustine then went on to warn people from interpreting said analogy as a perfect explanation of the Trinity, qualifying himself by stating that we can never know God, what is in Him, or what He Himself knows about Himself! Talk about getting yourself off the hook!

Analogies of the Trinity Concept

Analogies of every sort have been used by scholars and writers to try to explain the Trinity, from the idea that we can look at the three dimensions of space as one unit, yet each dimension is different in its own right. Or we can look at a pitchfork, with three prongs, each with its own sharpness, but all one pitchfork. Only when we hold in our minds the idea of the Trinity as three distinct persons, as in *people*, do we fail to see this symbolic image of three as one. That is where many people stumble with their interpretation, trying to continually distinguish a person from a personhood, or an individual being from an essence.

If all of this seems confusing (and a bit overwhelming), join the club! Despite all the texts, books, and works written on the Trinity throughout the centuries, modern Catholics today continue to believe in the simplicity of the Nicene Creed, in one God who exists as three persons ("person" as "an individual reality," not an individual human being). The Father, the Son, and the Holy Spirit are all one God in substance, each with its own distinction, but not divided—separate yet inseparable in a grander sense. This simple explanation, spoken aloud in churches all over the world, seems to summarize how some Christians today view the Trinity. They may not wish to delve any deeper into its profound and obscure meanings than this.

Confusing to say the least! The true and exact meaning of the Trinity, and how the three "parts" work alone and in unison, is still a matter of great discussion both in and out of the Christian church. Once you add on hundreds of years' worth of new ideas, new spin, and new directions, we have even more confusion! Not only religious motives, but political motives, helped to shape the understanding of the Trinity throughout the ages, shaped in accordance with the needs of the authorities, even if the populace understood it on a whole other level, as a personal measure of their faith. Though the Trinity has morphed in many directions, its core has fundamentally remained the same: three into one. One whole with three parts. Yet how those parts relate to the whole seems to be as evasive as ever.

Perhaps that is the biggest secret of the Trinity: that it is a mystery that can only be contemplated or understood on a deeper level than the intellect. Maybe there is another way entirely to look at this idea of three into one, a triune nature of anything, even of God—a nature understood only when we stop thinking in terms of persons and essences and personhoods and divine entities and look at the idea behind the Trinity in a different light.

Perhaps the soul alone knows what the secret is.

The Trinity Secret

2 The Logos of Creation: How the World Was Made

Who knows truly? Who here will declare whence it arose,
whence this creation?
—from the Rig Veda

Comparative cultural studies have now demonstrated
beyond question that similar mythic tales are to be found
in every quarter of this earth.
—Joseph Campbell, Myths to Live By

From the dawn of recorded history, humans have told stories about the creation of the world, and their place in it. Coded in parable, myth, and folklore, these creation stories had at their core the truth as each civilization knew and understood it, with their limited scientific acumen. They had no computers or high-powered telescopes, no modern technology to help them understand how the Universe came into existence. All they had was what they saw—what they observed. These observations became the creation myths, the Logos of Creation, that we know of today.

Much involves the imagination's ability to take what is observed and mold around it a story of how things work.

We do that today with our science fiction tales, imagining worlds bizarre and unknown, and creating for those worlds a history with a beginning, a middle, and often an end. Long ago, ancient civilizations sought to begin the story of their personal history by looking at the natural world around them, and constructing from that an archetype-filled myth steeped in symbolism and profound, hidden meaning. The creation or origin myth became the symbolic narrative of a people, from where they came, who they were, what they believed in, and how they saw the world around them. These stories were their identities, each showing how a specific culture or tradition came into being.

Many of these creation myths feature a distinct triune characteristic, as if the idea of a threefold process by which the Universe came into being was not the sole theory of one particular civilization. Primitive peoples as well spoke of a triune Universe, made up of worlds, or world levels, usually in threes, an idea that would spread into more sophisticated cultures and even into modern Christianity itself in the form of the Holy Trinity. This Trinity involves a creator, creation, and the act of creating. This is something that we will revisit in future chapters, but in terms of the origin of all that is, it is a simple explanation for how all that is came to be all that is. Intriguingly, origin stories are often grouped into three categories: those that suggest humans were always here on Earth; those that suggest humans were "created" from some entity or process; and those that suggest humans existed in another realm/world and were brought to this one. All, however, serve to try to answer the question: How did we, and everything else, get here?

Born out of Nothing

The worldview motifs often include the concept of a "world born out of nothing," a world that rises from the primordial waters, out of chaos and disorder. This nothingness from which everything seems to come is described in many ways: as an ocean that contains the seeds of all life, or a void from which the physical earth emerges. Out of the empty void springs forth physical manifestation. Out of the primordial chaos, order steps forth and worlds are born, Gods and Goddesses emerge, and eventually all forms of life evolve.

There has to be more than just an empty void, or swirling chaos, and then rich, varied life. There has to be a way, an action, an intention, or a mechanism that causes life to come forth out of nothingness. What triggers this sudden action? Why does it happen at all? What is the key that unlocks the door of potentiality and allows all of what we know as reality to be and to become?

In Genesis of the Old Testament, the world is born out of Logos, the Word. From nothing comes a word—a sound that resonates the world into existence. Then there is light and matter and form, and eventually life. The Word signifies the vibration of the God Force coming into being. This idea of speaking the world into existence shows up in the cosmogonies of many peoples all over the world. God in the Old Testament gives the command "Let there be light," but God already is. In the beginning was the Word and the Word was God. Humankind are created in the image of God, suggesting, as we will explore in a later chapter, that the same process by which we were created is also the process we use to create our reality, our existence.

In another form of Genesis, God breathes life into man, again a motif seen in other cosmogonies. In the Islamic tradition, which has similarities with the Judeo-Christian creation myth, the sky and earth are joined together, but then parted to take their individual shape or form. God, who in a six-day period creates all of life, plants, planets, and stars, does this. And when God is ready to create Man, He does so by first constructing an effigy of sorts, made of clay, earth, sand, and water, which He then "breathes" life into. This first man was called Adam. The Islamic creation myth closely follows the Judeo-Christian, with the creation of Eve, and the belief in a hierarchy of angels, including the proverbial bad boy, Lucifer.

The First Level

But what is God? What is this first level of the Trinity process? Is it all, or nothing at all?

The Logos of Creation

The void goes by many names, depending on the culture and tradition, but to all it is a place of pure potentiality that might be described as water, or darkness, or light, but always has a very primordial, even timeless, feel. This void is all that has ever existed before what we know of as reality came along. Yet it is also nothing in a sense that it has no discernable form or shape. Primordial soup. It is from this chaotic, yet infinite and timeless, ocean of all and nothing that the first deities emerged from—Gods and Goddesses that would control the rest of creation.

Other traditions would refer to a cosmic egg or flower, or a single Tree from which the branches of life emerged.

In Chinese philosophy, the fourth century BC text *Tao Te Ching* describes this void as "something featureless yet complete, born before heaven and earth." This formless void was named the Way, which interestingly birthed the concept of Unity, and then Duality, and then Trinity. Trinity then gave birth to the creatures of the world.

The Bakuba tribe in Africa believed the Earth was originally water and darkness, and that a giant named Mbombo ruled over the black void. Mbombo one day vomited up the sun, moon, and stars, and later vomited humans, animals, trees, and other necessities to the development of life as we know it. The Maasai of Kenya believed that humanity was originated by the Creator Enkai from a tree split into three separate pieces, each of which would be used to herd, cultivate, and hunt.

The Finnish people have their epic "Kalevala," which offers some of the usual elements: Chaos, primordial waters, the egg motif. Norse mythology begins with ice to the north, fire to the south, and in between a gap known as Ginnungagap, where melted ice and sparks of fire together began life. In Mandaeism, a monotheistic religion most prominent in Iraq, where it originated, creation begins with the supreme, formless entity that expresses itself through time and space as creation, spiritual as well as material. This entity then delegates to lower creators the actual production of the spiritual and material worlds, including the creation of the Cosmos in the image of Archetypal Man.

Often deities corresponded with cosmic bodies such as the sun or moon, or took on the form of animals or trees, always imbued with amazing powers and abilities, and yet, even faults and weaknesses. As deities, they then created humans and the "lower" forms of life that would proliferate upon the Earth.

The most popular myths of the Western world are the Greco-Roman myths, which follow the same creation process, but end up with Gods and Goddesses with different names. According to Hesiod's "Theogeny" (origin of Gods) it all began out of Chaos, nothingness, from which came light, Earth (Gaia), and Sky (Uranus). Gaia and Uranus birthed six sets of twins called Titans: Oceanus and Thethys, Coeos and Phoebe, Hyperion and Thea, Creos and Themis, Iapetos and Clymene, and Cronos and Rhea. (Names vary according to interpretations.) Gaia and Uranus also birthed three giant, multi-headed ugly Cyclopes. Apparently, even more chaos ensued when Uranus decided he was unhappy with his offspring and ordered them back into Gaia's womb. Gaia, of course, was pretty upset and vowed revenge against Uranus, calling upon her little Titans for help, and thus the legends we know of today were born, leading to the ultimate battle between the Olympians and Titans. (This is the abridged version!)

One interesting aspect occurs in the creation story told in Ovid's *Metamorphosis*, an abstract of which was translated by Mary M. Innes in *The Metamorphosis of Ovid*, which also begins with only chaos, described as lifeless, unorganized matter. At some point a God, or a natural higher force, begins to put the chaotic mass into order by separating it into components, then organizing into a harmonious whole. This organizing force or principal will be discussed more in future chapters, but again suggests that out of nothing, creation was formed, shaped, molded, categorized—all actions by which the Creator gives physicality to creation.

The Vedic Hindu tradition features a cosmic egg called Hiranyagarbha, which means "the golden embryo," from which the entirety of the Universe emerged. Later Hindu philosophy suggested a Trinitarian concept, called the Trimurti, of three governing entities; Brahma, Creator; Vishnu, Sustainer; and Shiva, Destroyer. Birth, life, and death. The Universe came into being from the cosmic egg because of one Word, the Aum/Om, which was considered a sacred sound with a resonant vibration of creative and generative power. This corresponds with the Word, Logos, of the Old Testament, and the power of sound

The Logos of Creation

and vibration to create physical reality, an idea also important to the Australian Aborigines, who believed that, as they walked and sang, they named the animals and creatures that populated their creations as they did, calling living things into being with music and song. Aborigines today take part in a ritual called Walkabout to retrace the steps and sing the songs of their ancestors as they created life.

Thus, sound, or resonance, was one critical mechanism by which the Creator was able to Create Creation, playing the vital second role of the Trinity—the activating agent, force, or action, required to manifest something from nothing. In the symbolism of the creation myth, this second role would belong to the deities that emerged from the chaos and void, which then used their powers to bring forth physical manifestation in the form of people, animals, and plants.

One of many Egyptian cosmogenies also includes the use of words to create physical reality out of the primordial waters. Atum-Raa acts as Supreme Being and utters specific words first to create the primordial water of Nu Naunet, which contains the embryos of all life. Again, Atum-Raa speaks more words to bring forth life in the form of an egg (the cosmic egg motif), and from the egg springs forth Raa, the Light, bringing life into existence ("Let there be light"). First the Word, then the Light, as in the Old Testament's Genesis story.

Another Egyptian creation tale also describes the eternal Ptah speaking the world and all its deities into form. The "Ennead" describes Atum rising out of the primordial water and creating Shu and Tefnet, moisture and dryness respectively, out of the seed of his semen (don't ask what he was doing at the time), who then birthed Geb and Nut, earth and sky. When separated, Geb and Nut's children became other deities representing life and death, including Isis and Osiris, who appear in many of the Egyptian stories. In the "Ogdoad," Ra takes the position as creator, emerging out of an egg or lotus due to the actions of four primordial forces. Ra takes Hathor as his wife (well, in this version he "created" her, much like the tale of Adam and Eve), and they have a son, Hor, who marries Isis, and so on and so on.

The Hermetic tradition of ancient Egypt, founded upon sacred literature written by an Egyptian sage, Hermes, around 3000 BC, has a detailed creation story. Hermes was so wise and honored he was called

"Trismegistus," which interestingly means "thrice great." Eventually Hermes would obtain Godlike status, and his writings would go on to influence not only ancient Egyptian and Greek philosophy, but modern-day Western thought as well, ranking the "Hermetica" (the name given to his writings) right up there with the *Tao Te Ching*, the Bible, and the Upanishads.

In the Hermetica, Hermes describes a mystical vision of the first act of creation. It all begins with Atum, the One-God, the Supreme Mind. Hermes asks Atum to show him the nature of reality. In a sort of reverse of sound first, light second, Hermes saw an all-embracing light—the Mind of God. He also sees dark, shadowy water, which becomes the unlimited potential from which the Universe is fashioned. There is an explosion of the Light, giving off energy, which cools to become the blackness of space. Into this blackness, the stars and planets will be born. Sounds a lot like the Big Bang, doesn't it?

From this "birth" of the Universe comes a sound, and the Light speaks a Word, calming chaos and serving as order and structure in the cosmos. Hermes calls this first Word the first thought in the Mind of God, or "the boundless Primal Idea, which is before the beginning."

I am that Light—the Mind of God, which exists before the chaotic waters of potentiality. My calming Word is the Son of God—the idea of beautiful order; the harmony of all things with all things. Primal Mind is parent of the Word, just as, in your own experience, your human mind gives birth to speech. They cannot be divided, one from the other, for life is the Union of Mind and Word.

Unlimited Field

This stunning concept might sound awfully familiar to those who have read *The Secret* or any Law of Attraction book or guide. It is also the basis for our new concept of the Trinity, as a process of creation, rather than a description of a deity. The idea that a thought in the Mind of God, placed upon the waters of unlimited potential, leads to physical manifestation is as old, apparently, as time itself. The unlimited potential itself speaks of later concepts like the Kingdom of Heaven, the

Akashic Fields, the Zero Point Field, Morphic Fields, even aether, as well as the behavior of particles and waves on the quantum level.

Hermes was way ahead of his time in terms of metaphysical thought; even in terms of scientific thought, for many of his descriptions of creation and the cosmos, and man's place in it, sound similar to scientific laws and quantum physics. His wisdom also served as a foundation for many of the religious and spiritual traditions to come in later years. The concept of the Mind of God as the Oneness that unites all is paralleled by the way our own human minds work, with varying levels of awareness and consciousness.

In *The Hermetica: The Lost Wisdom of the Pharaohs*, authors Timothy Freke and Peter Gandy state, "Hermes teaches that the mind of a human being is made in the image of God's Big Mind. If we can free our mind from the limitations imposed by the physical body, we can experience the Mind of God. We were created with the specific purpose of learning to do this." The authors go on to suggest that the expansion of awareness is the key. The modern study of Noetics, the power of the mind, thought, and intention, picks up where Hermes began. We have to give props to Hermes for developing some pretty profound metaphysical concepts that are coming back into vogue today. Truth is truth no matter what the time period.

Hermetic Influence of the Trinity

In terms of a Trinitarian view, we see the seeds of what might be the Father, Son, and Holy Spirit in Atum as God, Cosmos as creation, and Man as the third wheel. Yet all three are unified, just different parts of a whole—in essence, a unification of three individual "personas" or essences.

Recall the confusing description of the Christian Trinity on the Sacred Shield of the Trinity, upon which was transcribed:

- ✥ "The Father is God."

- ✥ "The Son is God."

- ✥ "The Holy Spirit is God."

The Trinity Secret

- "God is the Father."
- "God is the Son."
- "God is the Holy Spirit."
- "The Father is not the Son."
- "The Son is not the Father."
- "The Father is not the Holy Spirit."
- "The Holy Spirit is not the Father."
- "The Son is not the Holy Spirit."
- "The Holy Spirit is not the Son."

These myths often begin to sound like extended family trees, with higher deities birthing demi-Gods and then lower Gods, all the way down to the lowest forms of life. The need for humans to have a sense of ancestry obviously drove much of the mythology to include who begat whom. We all want to know where, and from whom, we came. And of course, we all then want to know why we act and behave the way we do—what makes us human and different from the animals we share the planet with. Some of the stories take on innumerable aspects that explain how things like good, evil, love, war, and even adultery came into existence, all a result of the actions of deities born out of the original All/Nothing.

The birth motif is popular throughout creation stories, suggesting that the storytellers themselves were mirroring what goes on in the Cosmos with their own birth, life, death cycles. Watching their own offspring being born, or seeing the birth of an animal, must have given them a pretty distinct idea of how "the lower forms of life" got here, even if they did not quite understand who or what made the Universe itself.

Another popular motif is water, the primordial soup from which all life emerges. We've mentioned many examples of this. Even the Native American traditions of the Cherokee, Creek, and Iroquois begin with nothing but water, or with the origins of earth being entirely underwater. Many Native American traditions such as the Seminole

The Logos of Creation

credit creation to a Godly Grandfather figure (something also seen in an Australian creation myth of the Great Father of All), or a trickster Raven (Inuit, Haida, Tlingit). Darkness is also popular, as it was to the Incan creation story, which begins with nothing but darkness from which emerges a God, Goddess, water, or light. The Navajo speak of the Holy Supreme Wind in the form of mists of light that permeated the darkness and animated the people found in three lower worlds. This legend also suggests that all existed first in a spiritual world before it did in the physical world, an important aspect of how creation works, even in our ordinary human lives.

Myth, Mind, and Trinity

Joseph Campbell is considered one of the most brilliant minds of the 20th century, and his books on mythology and comparative religion serve as the standard by which many universities teach said subjects to their students. His most well-known books include *Myths to Live By* and his classic study, *The Power of Myth*, both of which explore the connection between world mythology and the evolution of a Trinity Concept that would eventually make its way into Christology.

Campbell compares the triadic nature of Freud's id/ego/superego with terminology used in ancient myths to define the common themes and archetypes of the Hero's Journey as he recounts famous legends of Gilgamesh, as well as more current mythical legends in the making, such as Luke Skywalker of the *Star Wars* films. Campbell's extensive knowledge of religious history as well serves as an excellent resource for comparisons of the Trinity to the concept of Man's rise, fall, and redemption, rooted in ancient myth but later reborn in Western religions.

To Campbell, the idea of a Father, Son, and Holy Spirit served as a springboard for both understanding and actualization of enlightenment, as we authors also propose, and this concept of a tri-fold state of being turns up not just in creation myths, but even in later lore and legend surrounding the quest for the Holy Grail.

Earlier Hints of a Trinity

In Gerald A. LaRue's *Ancient Myth and Modern Life*, LaRue examines ancient myths as they pertain to modern humanity and life today, finding hints of the Trinity Concept in Sumerian cosmology and the divisions of primordial heaven and earth united as one creation. Aside from viewing the Trinity as an actual physical entity or a concept which serves to describe something tangible and visible (such as the creation of sky, earth, and water), LaRue points out several interesting references to the Trinity as *a state of being that advances the average man towards Divine Union*, evident in Egyptian hymns of the 14th century BC.

Contact with the Holy Spirit, thought by many to be only a Christian concept, occurs throughout the mythologies of Egypt all the way up to the dawn of Christianity, when myths of old seemingly gave way to a growing doctrine based upon a viable historical account of the life of Jesus Christ.

LaRue even dares explore what such powerful metaphysical symbolism like the Trinity Concept might mean for the future myths about to unfold in this new Millennium. Many people of many faiths see this current millennium as a time of both chaos and transformation, when the purpose and meaning of human existence may be redefined, birthing a new creation myth that matches the proverbial Phoenix rising from the ashes.

The Triune Nature of Creation

Although the triune nature of many creation myths is obvious (and we could not possibly include every myth from every tradition in one small chapter!), we can step away from cosmogenesis to cosmology, and again find several intriguing associations. If the cosmogenesis is the creation story or mythology of peoples, then the cosmology is their worldview. It is, quite simply, the study of the observable Universe as it is now, and humanity's place in it. Thus, the cosmology of modern humans will be quite different from that of their ancestors, who understood much less about the scientific aspects of the world they lived in than we do today. And yet, some motifs, archetypes, and symbols remain.

To the millions who follow Western religious traditions, the concept of a worldview holds, depending on your level of belief, that there is a heaven, hell, and purgatory. These worlds or levels of existence may have sub-levels, again depending on your specific sect, but we tend to believe that once we die, those are the choices. While here on earth, purgatory might be seen as physical existence—that in-between state where we spend our lives behaving in ways that will determine whether we end up in heaven, hell, or purgatory, where we will wait eternally for salvation that never comes.

A similar concept to heaven exists in the shamanic belief in three world levels, with the Upper World as a place inhabited by higher entities, divine beings, angels, and guides. The Lower World is where archetypal instinct rules, in the form of power animals and forces that can either help or harm us. In between lies the Middle World of common experience and reality. A shaman can travel between the three worlds to access information, heal the sick, and retrieve power animals or lost or broken souls. Traditionally, shamans use sound, in the form of rhythmic drumming or rattling, to alter the state of consciousness of one who will then journey through a dark tunnel into the non-reality of the Lower World to find a power animal, or rise to the Upper World to ask for wisdom from a higher guide. The hypnotic sounds of the drums and rattles keep the journey going until the desired goal is achieved, whether a healing recipe or answer to a pressing question. As the drums and rattles slow, the journey comes to an end, with the shaman returning to the reality of the Middle World.

Some southeastern Cherokee, who believe that the Cosmos is divided into the Upper World, This World, and the Lower World, share this concept of three world levels. This brings up an interesting thought. Obviously the nature of creation and reality had similarities that were naturally intuitive to a variety of cultures and peoples, no matter how far apart they existed. Remember that there was no Internet in those days, so similar worldviews speak highly of knowledge that was inherent to humans as a species, and the way those people accessed that shared storehouse of knowledge was often the same.

Rhythmic stimulation via song, sound, chanting, or drumming produces physiological changes in the central nervous system by affecting electrical activity in the sensory and motor regions of the brain. Native Americans often achieve similar results through drumming, dancing, and chanting. Movement and sound are tools for altering consciousness to allow for explorations of other world levels one does not normally access in the waking state.

For the shamans, these tools serve to transport them to the Upper World or Lower World, depending upon their needs or the needs of the one they journey for. The most adept shamans can recall in entirety what happens during a journey, despite being in a different conscious state.

The concept of heaven, hell, and earth could simply have come from basic observation. Heaven was the blue sky at day, the starry sky at night, unreachable yet always overhead. Earth was where life was lived. Hell? The fear of mortality and death must have driven our ancestors to create a negative to the positive of heaven. For with light there must be darkness. For with good there must be evil.

In heaven, the sky Gods ruled. In Sumerian mythology, Anu was a sky God, the God of heaven, which as a concept was later assimilated into the mythology of the Babylonians and Assyrians. Anu was the first in a figure of three Gods, including Bel and Ea, and became known as the father or king of all Gods (think the Father in the Trinity). Respectively, Bel controlled Earth, and Ea controlled the waters. Some scholars suggest that Anu, Bel, and Ea also represented the three zones of the ecliptic as the northern, middle, and southern zones. This triad concept was to be found in a number of worldviews, as if the number 3 held some profound importance in the creation of manifest reality and the deities, humans, and creatures that reality encompassed.

In Norse mythology, there are nine worlds divided into three levels. The Upper Level is the land of the Gods, of Asgard, and of the elves. The Middle Level is home to humans and giants, dark elves and dwarves. The Lower Level is home to a fiery and hot world in the southern region that mirrors the concept of hell. It is also home to the dead. These divisions of worlds sound similar to the three worlds of shamanism. In Norse legend, the world tree, Yggdrasil, holds the three levels together. This massive ash tree was considered sacred and said to bind the known world, and support the Universe. It had three roots that reached to each of the three levels. In some legends, the Lower Level is a world not of fire, but of ice and darkness—a place of the dead. Along with the three roots, three springs fed water to the world tree. Yggdrasil is first mentioned in the 13th-century *Prose Edda*, written by Snorri Sturluson, but scholars suggest it came from much earlier sources.

Though the world tree is a motif of other mythologies, including the Hungarian, Mongol, Siberian, Slavic, and Finnish, it is most prominent in Norse mythology. The world tree motif is also an integral part of the tradition and mythology of the Mayan, Aztec, and other Meso-American cultures, although they associated it with the four cardinal directions.

Fig. 2-1

The pagan beliefs of the Norse people included a special reverence for the triad, which is found throughout their mythology:

- Three distinct races of giants: mountain, frost, fire.
- Three original entities: primordial cow, Audhumla; first giant, Ymir; and first God, Buri.

The Trinity Secret

- ✽ Yggdrasil had three roots and three springs: see above.

- ✽ Three brothers create the world: Odin, Vili, Ve.

- ✽ Odin became the ruler of the third generation of Gods and had three special possessions: his spear, Gungnir; his golden ring, Draupnir; and his eight-legged horse, Sleipnir.

- ✽ Thor, another Norse God, uses three weapons against giants: his hammer, Mjolnir; his magical belt; and a pair of iron gauntlets that allow him to wield his mighty hammer.

- ✽ Odin spent three nights with a giantess named Gunnold, who gave him three drinks of mead out of three vessels.

- ✽ Freyr has three magical items: a ship, Skidbladnir; a boar, Gullinbursti; and a sword that can fight on its own.

- ✽ Freyja possessed three special artifacts: the necklace Brisingamen, a cloak that allows her to take the form of a falcon, and a chariot drawn by a pair of cats.

- ✽ At the Temple of Uppsala, there were three statues of Odin, Thor, and Freyr.

- ✽ Bifrost, the rainbow bridge that connected Yggdrasil to the other worlds, is three colors and is also known by three names.

- ✽ Heimdall, the guardian of rainbow bridge, has three special powers.

- ✽ The giant God Loki has three offspring by the giantess Angrboda: the wolf Fenrir, the World Serpent Jormungandr, and Hel.

- ✽ There are three Norms, or Goddesses of destiny: Urd—Fate, Verdani—Present, and Skuld—Future.

These are just a few of the examples of the prevalence of the number 3 in Norse lore. The number 9 held a special place as well.

The Logos of Creation

Threes Abound in Myth

Three rulers of three worlds are also found in Greek myth, with Zeus as ruler of the sky, Hades as ruler of the underworld, and Poseidon as ruler of the oceans. There were also three Graces, followers of the Goddess of love, Aphrodite, and Three Fates of Roman mythology. And the tripod was sacred to the Greek God Apollo. The Oracle at Delphi, Pythia, was said to sit upon a tripod before going into a trance. Cerberus was a three-headed watchdog that held guard over the underworld, never allowing anyone to get back to the land of the living.

The Mayan creation myth states that there were three attempts to create humans, the first out of clay, but was destroyed by flood; the second of wood, but was washed away by a terrible storm; and the third and finally successful attempt from maize, from which all humans are descended. Maize was an important staple to many native cultures, and became an archetypal symbol of abundance.

Pagan Triads

The importance of the triad to pagans throughout ancient times continues even in the more modern practices of paganism and witchcraft with the triune Maiden, Mother, Crone. These three aspects of the Goddess, which appear in a number of forms in many religions, were recognized as three ages of womanhood, but also the greater complexity of humanhood in general. Like the Holy Trinity, the triune Goddess was one entity, with three distinct facets. The maiden represents birth and youth, a time of fecundity and fruitfulness. The Mother was the maturity of motherhood, nourishing and caring, matronly, and the time associated with midlife. The Crone was old age, wisdom, and experience, and was actually revered and not treated with the disgust old age is in modern culture. The Crone was the culmination of the triune Goddess, with all her life experience, knowledge, strength, and fortitude, as well as her preparation for the next cycle of birth, life, and death.

Maiden-Mother-Crone imagery was also said to represent the three phases of the moon: full, waning, and new or dark moon. This same concept is found in the Celtic Fate as the Three Norns representing the full, waning, and new moon: Mani, Nithi, and Nyi. Again, by observing nature, various cultures created symbology that mirrored those of other cultures thousands of miles away. What we could not understand, we "deitized," in reverence, awe, and even sometimes fear.

The African Ashanti is a moon Goddess depicted as three people, two black and one white. The Roman Goddess Diana, revered in pagan traditions, was a triple Goddess of a different nature, ruling the hunt, the moon, and the underworld. The Arabic Goddess Manant is a threefold Goddess representing the three Holy Virgins, Al-Itab, Al-Uzza, and Al-Manat. The Celtic Goddess Minerva is often portrayed alongside the two Gods Apollo and Mercury, suggesting a more co-ed triune divinity! The moon God of the Slavic tradition is triple-headed. The Celts revered the number 3, and their mythology is also ripe with examples, such as the three Brigids (threefold Goddess Brigit), three Blessed Ladies, the three trees that make up the faery triad (oak, ash, and thorn), and the shamanic belief in three overlapping worlds of past, present, and future.

The Number 9 and Enneads

Another popular motif is the division of nine into three groups of three, which occurs in the Egyptian account of creation, with the "Ennead," a group of nine divinities, and the triad of divine Father, Mother, and Son. Each temple in Egypt had its own ennead and triad, the most widely known and revered being the ennead of Ra and his offspring.

In Christianity, the numbers 9 and 3 are sacred, with 9 representing the divine nature of the Trinity tripled—333. The number 9 then becomes the highest level of the triune nature of life and creation. The interesting thing about the number 9 is that if you multiply anything by 9 and then add up the digits of the sum, you always get 9!

- $1 \times 9 = 9$
- $2 \times 9 = 18$ and $1+8 = 9$

The Logos of Creation

- 𝕏 3 x 9 = 27 and 2 + 7 = 9
- 𝕏 4 x 9 = 36 and 3 + 6 = 9
- 𝕏 5 x 9 = 45 and 4 + 5 = 9

And so on and so on and so on….

3 Times 3: The Number 9 as the Mathematical Finger Print of God?

The intriguing work of a man named Marko Rodin has many looking to the number 9, or the tripled 3, as the Finger Print of God. Rodin has developed Vortex-Based Mathematics, a complex system based upon what he claims is the "underpinning geometry of the universe, the fabric of time itself." His discovery of amazing number patterns serves as the foundation of what he suggests is a perfect description for how energy flows. His dynamic system of mathematics involves the number 9 as a profound numerical marvel that stands for Abha, the Great Name of God in the Bahai Faith, using a number-alphabet correlation. The number 9 also serves as the link and the "control" between the dualism of Yin and Yang, as the S-curve between the two halves that form a trinary, symbolizing the concept that everything in the universe is based on thirds, and not dualities. "The number 9 is Energy being manifested in a single moment event of occurrence in our physical world of creation…. It is the singularity or the primal point of Unity…." He even suggests that the number 9 is the missing particle in the universe known as Dark Matter."

Fascinating work, which can be delved into more deeply at *www.markorodin.com.*

Thoth and the Legend of the Emerald Tablets

We will continue to look at the importance of the number 3 in a future chapter—and trust us, it shows up everywhere—but first we want

The Trinity Secret

to compare more modern religious belief systems and their understanding of the Trinity, or the triune nature of the divine process of creation. We would first like to offer some intriguing words from a mysterious text called *The Emerald Tablets of Thoth the Atlantean*, which were translated in the early 20th century by an equally mysterious man named Dr. M. Doreal, who discovered the texts in the pyramids of South America. The writings have become an esoteric "legend" and speak of the wisdom of Thoth/Hermes in tablets that cover the keys to wisdom, time, space, magic, cause and effect, above and below, life and death, and more. They can be found online on a number of Websites.

Thoth is associated with Hermes, considered to be Hermes Trismegistus in his next incarnation. Thoth was a master and king and a teacher in ancient Egypt, and is deified as the God of Wisdom in ancient esoteric Egyptian circles. In the Emerald Tablets, Thoth writes about the legendary civilization of Atlantis and of its highly advanced civilization. Thoth focused on the spiritual and mystical beliefs—actually, knowledge—these Atlanteans possessed, a knowledge that allowed them to fulfill their destiny and become higher, divine beings. When those who would use this power for evil got hold of this metaphysical knowledge of spiritual transformation, they set about to use it and triggered the destruction of Atlantis. Thoth moved to Egypt with other divinely evolved Atlanteans and, according to Plato, helped teach Egyptians geometry, astronomy, and writing.

There also exists a text called *The Secret of Hermes* or *The Emerald Tablet of Hermes Trismegistus* (which some allege is the same text as *The Emerald Tablets of Thoth,* and others suggest is a different translated text altogether), which became the foundation of European alchemy. It is a brief text that has been translated into numerous languages. The oldest source is the *Kitah Sirr-al-Asrar,* which serves to offer advice to Arabic rulers in a form of a letter from Aristotle to Alexander the Great. Two Latin translations allege to be the most accurate, including the *Secretum Secretorum* (*Secrets of Secrets*) by Johannes Hispaniensis circa 1140. This text is often credited as influencing author Rhonda Byrne to write the mega-popular Law of Attraction book *The Secret.* It also influenced the teachings and writings of both medieval and Renaissance alchemists in search of the key to transmutation, and others commented or translated the text with their own special spin, including Roger Bacon, Aleister Crowley, Albertus Magnus, and even Sir Isaac Newton, who also had a fascination with alchemy.

The tablets of Hermes have been regarded as containing the necessary "recipe" for alchemical gold, including the necessity of adjusting one's consciousness to a higher degree. The alchemist might transmute lead into gold, but to truly be successful he must also transmute his lower self into a higher self. This association with evolving the individual state of consciousness to create "gold" is really the basis for all Law of Attraction teachings to follow. We'll explore those concepts in more detail later.

Following is the contemporary Latin translation:

1. [It is] true, without error, certain and most true,
2. That which is below is as that which is above, and that which is above is as that which is below, to perform the miracles of the one thing.
3. And as all things were from the one, by means of the meditation of the one, thus all things were born from the one, by means of adaptation.
4. Its father is the Sun, its mother is the Moon, the Wind carried it in its belly, its nurse is the earth.
5. The father of the whole world [or "of all of the initiates"?] is here.
6. Its power is whole if it has been turned into earth.
7. You will separate the earth from the fire, the subtle from the dense, sweetly, with great skill.
8. It ascends from earth into heaven and again it descends to the earth, and receives the power of higher and of lower things.
9. Thus you will have the Glory of the whole world.
10. Therefore will all obscurity flee from you.
11. Of all strength this is true strength, because it will conquer all that is subtle, and penetrate all that is solid.

12. Thus was the world created.
13. From this were wonderful adaptations, of which this is the means. Therefore am I named Thrice-Great Hermes, having the three parts of the philosophy of the whole world.
14. It is finished, what I have said about the working[s] of the Sun.

Much more is spoken of the secret of secrets in the Thoth tablets. We were particularly drawn to Tablet XV: Secret of Secrets, for its description of the "mystery of nature." That and a certain number that kept popping up again and again and again.

Hear ye now of the mystery of nature,
the relations of life to the Earth where it dwells.
Know ye, ye are threefold in nature,
physical, astral and mental in one.
Three are the qualities of each of the natures;
nine in all, as above, so below.

In the physical are these channels,
the blood which moves in vortical motion,
reacting on the heart to continue its beating.
Magnetism which moves through the nerve paths,
carrier of energies to all cells and tissues.
Akasa which flows through channels,
subtle yet physical, completing the channels.
Each of the three attuned with each other,
each affecting the life of the body.
Form they the skeletal framework through
which the subtle ether flows.
In their mastery lies the Secret of Life in the body.
Relinquished only by will of the adept,
when his purpose in living is done.
Three are the natures of the Astral,
mediator is between above and below;
not of the physical, not of the Spiritual,
but able to move above and below.

The Logos of Creation

Three are the natures of Mind,
carrier it of the Will of the Great One.
Arbitrator of Cause and Effect in thy life.
Thus is formed the threefold being,
directed from above by the power of four.
Above and beyond man's threefold nature
lies the realm of the Spiritual Self.

From another interpretation we found this:

Three are the qualities of God in His Light-Home: Infinite power,
Infinite Wisdom, Infinite Love.

Three are the powers given to the Masters: to transmute evil,
assist good, use discrimination.

Three are the powers creating all things: Divine Love possessed
of perfect knowledge, Divine Wisdom knowing all possible means,
Divine Power possessed by the joint Will of Divine Love and Wisdom.

We, the authors, cannot verify the accuracy of the interpretations of these texts, or who composed or originated them, as with the holy texts and wisdom teachings of every religion and spiritual tradition, but we found them fascinating enough to mention in this chapter. Why is the number 3 so *important* to so many cultures in terms of describing not only the nature of God, but of us lowly humans as well? Could we, also, be like God? Whether we speak of the lore of creation, the accounts passed down from our ancestors of how we, as humans, came to exist, or we talk of the natural world and its cosmic laws and forces around us in terms of archetype, symbol, and myth, the number 3 is woven throughout the story of us. From the origin of the Universe itself to the creation of humankind, the triad appears over and over, beckoning us to understand its true meaning. Wisdom tells us all good things come in threes.

Born in the image. As Above, So Below.

The Trinity Secret

3 Triads, Triads, and More Triads

There are three classes of people: Those who see. Those who see when they are shown. Those who do not see.
—Leonardo da Vinci

Human behavior flows from three main sources: desire, emotion, and knowledge.
—Plato

As we now understand, the concept of the Trinity did not originate with Christianity. In fact, every major and minor religious system has a similar triadic concept that describes the nature of reality in spiritual terms. Only semantics separate these worldwide concepts from what could be termed as a "spiritual unified theory" that can be explored and embraced by all people, no matter what their claimed religion or belief system.

To Joseph Campbell, the idea of a Father, Son, and Holy Spirit served as a springboard for both understanding and actualization of enlightenment, and this concept of a tri-fold state of being turns up even in the oldest recorded wisdom

teachings on earth. Campbell's focus was on examining the commonalities of religions and even myth, and this idea was not lost on him. The
Trinity was everywhere.

The Hermetic Connection

About 3,000 years before the birth of Christ, the Egyptian sage
Hermes wrote a classic piece of sacred literature called *The Hermetica*.
This wisdom teaching of the ancient pharaohs influenced much of
Egyptian, Greek, and even modern Western thought and civilization,
vaulting Hermes to the status of a God, and the reverent title of
"Trismegistus," meaning "Thrice Great."

Hermetic thought may have even served as the foundation for
Christianity. St. Augustine remarked in *Retractions*, "That which is
called the Christian religion existed among the ancients, and never
did not exist." Thus, the ideas and concepts expressed by the "Thrice
Great" set the stage for the future teachings of many great religions.

Hermes believed that God was one Big Mind, and that everything
that existed was a thought within the Mind of God. This Mind was an
Oneness that united everything, and, most importantly, we could access
that Mind anytime. He also taught that the nature of everything was
threefold; even man:

There are then these three—
Atum, Cosmos, man.
The Cosmos is contained by Atum.
Man is contained by the Cosmos.
The Cosmos is the son of Atum.
Man is the son of the Cosmos,
And the grandson, so to speak, of Atum.

Notice the use of the word *Atum*, which is the first, according
to Hermes, and parallel with the name of the "first man" in the Old
Testament—Adam.

Hermes goes on to say, "The Maker made man to govern with him, and if man accepts this function fully, he becomes a vehicle of order in the Cosmos." Being both spirit and matter, man was considered the intermediary between these two great principles; much like the role the Holy Spirit plays in the traditional Trinity.

From the Gnostic Gospels of Christianity, much more can be gleaned about this concept, as undertaken by Elaine Pagels in her landmark study of these ancient and most sacred texts, *The Gnostic Gospels*, in which we learn that the early Christian concepts of the Trinity were molded from Judaic terminology for the description of a genderless God, later "masculinized" by the Christians.

Karen Armstrong, in her stunning and scholarly book *The History of God*, continues the controversy over the molding of the Westernized Trinity as she presents a battle over semantics and interpretation that exploded in the ninth century AD, when Celtic philosopher Erigena challenged Augustine's rather anthropomorphic Trinity view of Three-Persons-in-One-God with his far more philosophical views of God as Nothing and Everything. Meanwhile, as Armstrong accounts, the Christian Church leadership struggled to maintain control of the doctrine it would present to the public, including a comprehensible interpretation of the Trinity as the personas of God, despite the resistance of many who refused or simply were not capable of seeing God as any structure or "personage."

Leaving Christianity behind for a moment, research into the Trinity leads us to other major religious texts, such as the Tao Te Ching, Bhagavad-Gita, Kabbalah, and *Tibetan Book of the Dead*. These texts all serve to provide unusual insights into how this concept of a threefold nature of God and our union with the Divine is seen and understood in different religious systems.

In the *Tibetan Book of the Dead*, we learn of the "Three Bodies of Buddhahood," a basic concept of the triadic levels of existence: "A person must therefore be responsible for herself on all three levels. As Buddhahood, the triad becomes the Three Buddha Bodies, ordinary body becoming the Emanation Body, speech the Beatific Body, and the mind the Truth Body."

Triads, Triads, and More Triads

These three Buddha Bodies correlate with body, mind, and spirit, and with the concept of the Father as God, the Son as personhood, and the Holy Spirit as the process by which a person becomes one with God.

We even see parallels in the "Three Jewels" or "Three Treasures" of the *Buddha*, the *Dharma* (law or action), and the *Sangha* (community). The Jains refer to this same Trinity as *samyag-darsana* (correct insight), *samyag-jnana* (correct knowledge), and *samyag-caritra* (correct conduct)—again, the spirit, mind, body triad as a process toward an enlightened life.

Trikaya: Three Bodies or Personalities

Trikaya is a Sanskrit word for the three levels of Buddhahood. Also known as the Bodies or Personalities of Buddha, these three aspects are all simply different forms of one truth, the Dharma:

1. Nirmanakaya—the physical body, the body of Buddha, an example being the body of Gautama Buddha.
2. Sambhogakaya—the reward body given when a bodhisattva completes vows.
3. Dharmakaya—the body of truth itself; transcends physical and spiritual bodies. The Absolute.

The Trikaya teaches both the nature of reality and the nature of the Buddha. There is a mention of a fourth Buddha body, the Svabhavikakaya, which means "essential body" in the Vajrayana Buddhist teachings. Vajrayana, by the way, originates from around the sixth century BC and is said to be one of three routes to enlightenment, the other two being Hinayana and Mahayana. Other Buddhist scholars suggest the three paths or "vehicles" of Buddhism are the Hinayana, Mahayana, and Tantrayana.

Vietnamese Buddhist monk Thich Nhat Hanh, in his beautiful book *Living Buddha, Living Christ*, offers extensive comparisons of Western and Eastern thought in regards to the Trinity.

After meeting with Christian clergy, Hanh remarked, "I told the priest that I felt all of us have the seed of the Holy Spirit in us, the capacity of healing, transforming, and loving. When we touch that seed, we are able to touch God the Father and God the Son."

Hanh powerfully presents the idea of the Trinity as the way to direct knowing of the Divine that transcends all religious labels and names. He claims the safest way to approach the Holy Spirit is through the concept of mindfulness, and that "someone animated by the energy of the Holy Spirit…is the Son of Man and the Son of God"—a concept not alien to Buddhists who are familiar with the nature of non-duality.

The Buddhist Trinity of Buddha, Dharma, and Sangha sounds very much like what Christian doctrine teaches, yet presents the Trinity as more accessible to all followers. Many Christian churches hold the Holy Spirit over the heads of their followers like a threatening specter that picks and chooses whom it will "descend" upon. Not in Buddhism, where we learn that the spirit is the breath of life itself and that it is available to everyone.

A parallel to this can be found in The Bhagavad-Gita, which states in its Eighteenth Teaching:

There is no being on earth
or among the gods in heaven
free from the triad of qualities
that are born of nature.

In his introduction to Barbara Stoler Miller's translation of the Gita, Huston Smith states:

To uncover the nature of the self, the Gita approaches it from three directions that triangulate the self…. One of these concerns its makeup, its attributes or qualities. A second distinguishes different spiritual attitudes that serve as starting points for the journey to God…the third system of classification turns on differences in what grabs people's interests in the world.

Triads, Triads, and More Triads

All three attributes, per Huston Smith, create a model of the human self and his psychological and spiritual nature.

Even the various aspects of Krishna's material nature are described as triadic and are analyzed in terms of the three fundamental qualities of lucidity (*sattva*), passion (*rajas*), and dark inertia (*tamas*). These three natural qualities are what constitute, in Hindu thought, the nature of man. Note here the similarities to the id, ego, and superego concept of Freud!

One can even see a parallel here with the later Christian concept of heaven, hell, and purgatory.

The triadic nature of Hindu faith is also made up of these three elements, inherent in the embodied self, and this Trinity of lucidity, passion, and dark inertia presents itself throughout the Gita as a symbol of the three levels of man's physical and spiritual nature.

In the *Tao Te Ching*, the centerpiece of all Chinese religion and philosophy, we see a close parallel between the Tao teaching of *te* (individual soul), *Tao* (universal or cosmic soul), and *chi* (universal energy) and the older Hindu Vedic concept of *atman* (individual soul), *Brahman* (universal soul), and *Moksha* (liberation). *Tao* and *Brahman* both represent Cosmic Unity, or the Father. The individual soul as represented by *te* and *atman* can also be called the Son. And as for the Holy Spirit, we offer *chi* energy present in all things, or, for the Vedic Hindus, a pure liberation or freedom of the soul. The Tao teachings of the Yan Hui, one of Confucius's disciples, also include the idea that the human being and cosmos share three life-forces: spirit (*shen*), breath (*qi*), and vital essence (*jing*), also known as the "Three Pure Ones."

Eastern Trinity Influences

This personification of the triadic nature of being is echoed in every wisdom tradition from the East, with only slight variations in presentation and semantics.

Chinese Buddhism also presents the Trinity Concept as the Three Jewels—Buddha, Dharma, and Sangha, or the Godhead, his teachings, and his community (also referred to as the Teacher, His Teaching, and the freedom the teachings inspire). These three jewels symbolized the actions to be taken to achieve union with the divine.

Thus the concept of Buddha as a physical entity (although definitely *not a god!*), Dharma as a physical reality of right action, and Sangha as a physical community or the "body of man" is transformed into symbols of inner transformation, where the inner God uses inner right thought and action to achieve a community of spirit. This is what Hanh means when he emphasizes that we can "touch the living Buddha and the living Christ" within each of us.

Hanh also constantly refers to the parallels between Buddhist foundational practice of the Three Jewels of Buddha, Dharma, and Sangha and the Trinity of the Christian church. The common symbolism is not lost on Hanh, who suggests that just as taking refuge in the Three Jewels is at the foundation of every Buddhist practice, taking refuge in the Trinity is at the foundation of every Christian practice.

Buddhists and Hindus alike realized that whatever force drove the outer world also drove the inner world of the mind and consciousness. Deities in physical form also were deities in consciousness, as if Freud's id, ego, and superego were given actual names and faces within the mind.

Zen Buddhism takes this move away from a physical reality to a symbolic "reality" one step further, as suggested by third-century Confucian teacher and philosopher Xun Zi, who stated, "Heaven has its seasons, Earth has its riches, and Man has his culture. This is what is meant by the Trinity." Zi understood that the importance of humankind in the Universe was "equal to, but different from" the importance of heaven and earth. Humanity's purpose was to utilize the resources of heaven and earth to create its own culture, guided by rules of morality and ethics.

The Dawn of Christian Trinitarian Thought

As the dawn of Christianity unfolded further to the West, the Trinity, once created as a description for the physical reality of God, the Christ, and the divine life-giving Breath, was also evolving into a more spiritual symbol. Ancient Aramaic, the language of Jesus himself, suggests that the Holy Spirit was really Holy Breath. The Aramaic language had only one word for "spirit," which also meant "breath," "wind," and "air." Thus the term *Rehab d'Qoodsha*, which referred to the Source of Breath, also meant Holy Breath, which, when accessed by humanity, led to union with *Alaha*, the One Being.

The early fathers of the Christian Church grappled with a way to keep the idea intact that one could only know God "through" a pope, bishop, or priest, and not directly on his or her own, while at the same time offering a description of the Trinity that laypeople could understand. The metaphysical symbolism of the Holy Trinity was something the Church fathers could not deny, for hadn't Jesus Himself said, "For behold, the Kingdom of God is within you" (Luke 17:21) and "I and the Father are One" (John 10:30)? Even Job of the Old Testament had stated, "But truly it is the spirit in a mortal, the breath of the Almighty, that makes for Understanding" (32:8) and "The spirit of God hath made me, and the breath of the Almighty hath given me life" (33:4). Statements such as these are abundant throughout the Old Testament and New Testament, and their emphasis on the union of man and God through the work of the Holy Spirit could not be ignored.

Gregory of Nyssa explained in the *Philosophical Dictionary* that "the divine nature is unnamable and unspeakable"—that "Father, Son and Spirit are only terms that we use" to speak of the "*energeiai*" by which the Divine can be made known. He goes on to state "these terms have symbolic value because they translate the ineffable reality into images that we can understand."

"Men have experienced God as transcendent (the Father, hidden in accessible light), as creative (the Logos) and as immanent (the Holy Spirit)," Karen Armstrong writes in her 1994 book, *A History of God*. "The Trinity, therefore, should not be seen as a literal fact but as a paradigm that corresponds to real facts hidden in the life of God."

Because this image of the Holy Trinity as a mystical or spiritual symbol or experience made more sense than the image of a physical reality, many orthodox churches accepted the Trinity as an inspiring religious experience. Other more Westernized denominations continued to struggle with the baffling Trinity, and began to move away from the literal interpretation toward a more theoretical and experiential interpretation, the result, says Armstrong, of *theoria*, or contemplation.

Perhaps it was the Greeks more than any group that challenged the Augustinian perception of the Trinity as three persons within a whole Unity. The Greeks had always believed that the true reality of God's nature was beyond human understanding or description, and that the more Latin descriptions made the Trinity too rational, rather than Spiritual. Greek Orthodox churches would be instrumental in using the Trinity as a central point of their identification of the Divine. Western churches would eventually drop the baffling Trinity altogether from their doctrine during the Enlightenment period of the 18th century, complaining that the Three-Persons-in-One-God theory did not make sense, although to the Greeks it made total sense when taken at a symbolic, not literal, level.

Triple-Powered Goddess

This beautiful prayer, "Papyri Graecae Magicae," to the Greek lunar Goddess Selene, daughter of the Titans Hyperion and Theia, was written in the fourth century AD and is a perfect example of the divine reverence of the number 3 when depicting deities.

Triple-headed, triple-voiced Selene
Triple-Pointed, triple-faced, triple-necked,
And goddess of the triple ways, who hold
Uniting flaming fire in triple baskets,
And who oft frequent the triple way
And rule the triple decades.

The Gnostic Trinity

Meanwhile, Gnostic Christian texts would bring the feminine face of God into the fray. Elaine Pagels recounts a passage from "The Apocryphon of John" that tells of a mystical vision of the Trinity he experienced while grieving for the Crucified Christ: "…and I was afraid, and I saw in the light…a likeness with multiple forms, and the likeness had three forms." John questions the vision and receives this answer: "I am the one who is with you always. I am the Father; I am the Mother; I am the Son."

Pagels explains that this version of the Trinity is based upon the Hebrew term for spirit, *ruah*, which is a feminine word, thus concluding that the feminine "person" conjoined with the Father and Son must be the Mother. Another feminine Trinity symbol appears in the Gospel of Philip, which describes the Holy Spirit as Mother and Virgin, consort to the Heavenly Father. Philip believes this is the true account for the virgin birth symbolism of Christology. "Christ, therefore, was born from a virgin," meaning from the Holy Spirit, not from a virgin woman named Mary.

Pagels also suggests that Wisdom (Sophia) could also have served as the feminine aspect of the Trinity. Sophia, wisdom, translates a Hebrew feminine term (*hokmah*) and refers to the saying in Proverbs "God made the world in Wisdom."

Another powerful Gnostic text that suggests a feminine aspect of the Trinity is the poem "Thunder, Perfect Mind," which most scholars agree was written by a woman (although it is not known whom). "I am the first and the last.… I am the whore, and the holy one.… I am the wife and the virgin.… I am godless, and I am one whose God is great." This parallels another text, the *Trimorphic Protennoia* (*Triple-formed Primal Thought*), discovered from the famed Nag Hammadi site. This text proclaims the three feminine powers of Thought, Intelligence, and Foresight, and opens with the stunning lines "I am the Thought that dwells in the Light…she who exists before the All.… I am the Invisible One within the All.…"

Perhaps it is time to look upon the Trinity in a more feminine light as well, as the Mother, the Daughter, and the Holy Spirit!

The Kabbalah and the Trinity

Jewish mystics who studied the Kabbalah also understood the triadic symbolism of their Christian counterparts. It was the Hebrew God Yahweh, after all, that the early Christian Church was trying to define by adding the Trinitarian nature. In the Kabbalah, a more metaphysical understanding of the nature of God, the All, *Ein Sof*, takes form in the three major *sefirot*, or the qualities through which the Divine emanates and performs its actions. The first major emanation is *Keter*, called *Ayin* (nothingness). From Keter a second point emanates, *Hokmah* (wisdom), also called *Yesh* (being). This *sefirah* is the beginning of being-from-nothingness, the beginning of revelation and existence. The third point of emanation is *Binah* (understanding), which is required to reveal that which exists. From these three *sefirot* emerge the six dimensions of providence, from the *Hesed* (love) sefirah to the others below.

Each group of sefirot are revealed in triads from a sefirah before it. For example, *Hesed* (love) emanated from *Hokhmah* (wisdom); *Gevurah* (power) from *Binah* (understanding); and *Tif'eret* (beauty) from *Keter* (nothingness). Kabbalists claim that it is improper to probe the essence of the first three sefirot because they constitute the divine mind, wisdom, and understanding. Note the parallel here with the early Greek Christian Orthodox Church's claim that the true nature of the Divine was unexplainable, thus the need for a more symbolic interpretation of the Trinity.

Kabbalists understood the *Ein Sof* as the Infinite, from which all else emanated, including humankind. In "The Chain of Being" from *The Essential Kabbalah*, we are told, "The entire chain is one. Down to the last link, everything is linked with everything else; so divine essence is below as well as above, in heaven and on earth. There is nothing else." Then, in "*Ein Sof* and You" we learn that "Each of us emerges from the *Ein Sof* and is included in it. We live through its dissemination." The *Ein Sof* is the Father of the Christian world. We are the Sons. And the dissemination of the *Ein Sof* is the Holy Spirit that moves in and through us.

Triads, Triads, and More Triads

As Rabbi Eliezar ben Judah of Worms, Jewish mystic and philosopher, proclaimed in "The Song of Unity," in Gershom Sholem's *Major Trends in Jewish Mysticism*, "Everything is in Thee and Thou art in everything: Thou fillest everything and dost encompass it: when everything was created. Thou was in everything; before everything was created, Thou was everything." This is a concept we will be looking at from a more scientific perspective in an upcoming chapter, and offers a perfect example of how metaphysical and mystical ideas often are paralleled in science—but again, with much different language used to describe them.

Islamic Belief

Unlike its sister religions of Judaism and Christianity, Islam considered the Trinity a blasphemous concept. To the followers of the Koran, or Qur'an trying to speculate on things theological was referred to, somewhat condescendingly, as *Zanna*—self-indulgent guesswork about things that cannot possibly be known. The idea of a triadic nature of God was not something Muslims accepted, or would even consider. To the Muslim, God or *al-Lah* was all, is all, and will always be all there is.

Muhammad the Prophet, who channeled the Koran in a series of trance states, considered the Koran the word of God directly translated to Arabic and that what the Koran revealed was that God, *al-Lah*, was indivisible All. This emphasis on total oneness would turn the Islamic churches away from the Trinity doctrine being embraced in nearby Christian churches. According to Armstrong in *The History of God*, the Christian Incarnation of Christ was also blasphemous to the Islamic Church. Instead, the Koran spoke of an impersonal God who cannot be personified, but only glimpsed through signs of nature and contemplation of the Koran itself.

The Islamic Church, however, does believe in an experience of transcendence with the Ultimate Reality, by utilizing the Koran as a spiritual discipline, and it is in this context that we see a Trinity Concept. Muhammad, and any other Muslim devotee, surely could study the Koran and pray to *al-Lah* in a trance state, and experience this transcendence. This would suggest the man as the Son, the study of the Koran and prayer as the activating agents of the Holy Spirit, and *al-Lah*, of course, as the Father. In this sense alone do we see a Trinity evolve in the Islamic religion; otherwise the Koran more closely parallels an older Semitic concept of Divine Unity and refuses to accept that God can somehow "beget" a son. To the Muslim, there is no God but *al-Lah*, and no human-like being (such as Christ or Buddha) that can be a "part" of the Divine Nature. But admittedly, Muslims could develop a "sense" of the transcendent presence by study of the Koran, prayer, and devotion.

Eventually, even Islam would develop a more philosophical branch of mystics, known as the Sufis, who used chanting and prayer to achieve a union with the Divine that suggested the Divine could indeed be manifest in man. To the Sufis, much like the Kabbalists and Gnostic Christians, the distinction was made between the essence of God, and the God we glimpse in revelation and the creation around us. God is, and would always be, essentially unknowable, but the essence could be experienced, through prayer, through meditation, or, as with the Mawlawiyyah order of Sufis known as the "whirling dervishes," through concentrated dance and spinning to create a transcendent state in which the boundaries of self dissolve into union with the Divine. Thus, the worshipper uses a more metaphysical approach and becomes the Son who uses the trancelike spinning and dancing (or chanting, praying, bowing, and so forth) as the means of inviting in the Holy Spirit (expanding consciousness while breaking down ego boundaries) to become one with the Father (*al-Lah*, Divine Essence).

The Metaphysical Trinity

Modern-day Christians and non-Christians alike share in the understanding of a metaphysical Trinity. New Thought religions of the current day and age, including Unity Christianity and Religious Science, are built upon the foundation of divine union as a direct experience of God accessible to anyone. Ernest Holmes, founder of Religious Science, teaches in his masterpiece text, *The Science of Mind*, that the Christ indwells our own lives, and without Him we can do nothing. He likens the inner Christ to the Holy Spirit that moves in and through us, guiding and directing our lives: "The Christ Spirit comes to all alike, proclaiming Itself as the Son of God...."

Holmes suggests a triadic nature for the unity of God and man—the spirit, soul, and body. He uses the terms Universal Spirit for the Father, Universal Subjectivity for the Holy Spirit or soul of the Universe, and Manifest Universe for the Body of God and all its sons and daughters therein. "So we find that man is one with everything in the physical world; one with the Soul of the Universe in the subjective world; and one with the Spirit of God in the conscious mind." This Trinitarian theory of man's Divine Nature also has strong parallels to the Freudian concept of three levels of conscious being: id, ego, and superego.

Sigmund Freud, considered the "father of psychoanalysis," described the id as the primal or initial principle of life—the pleasure principle. The id was the lowest rung on the ladder of the organization of personality. This was the locale of impulse, as the primary subjective reality that exists before an individual is exposed to the experiences of the world. The ego described the level of being in which a person transacts with the world. The ego is governed by reality, that which exists, and is the connector between the id and superego (sort of the psychological Holy Spirit connecting Son to Father). The superego is the third major level of personality, the moral/judicial branch, so to speak—where a person's moral code is based. The superego is the ideal consciousness, the ego at its best, more focused on striving for perfection than for the reality of the ego and the pleasure of the id.

This is a very simplified description of the work of Freud, but it clearly corresponds with the triadic symbolism we find in religion and spirituality, of three levels of being and three levels of the nature of the Divine—with a basic primal level, a middle level of action and process, and a top level of transcendence and "perfection." The irony here is that Freud himself regarded belief in God as an illusion that mature people should let go of! He felt God was simply an infantile projection of the desires for a loving, protective Father, and for fairness and justice and eternal life. Still, his own imagery of the inner workings of personality so closely parallel the Trinity Concept of the nature of the Divine, one has to wonder if he truly believed his own proclamations!

Many of his contemporaries did not quite fully agree with him, including Alfred Adler, who believed God to be a projection of humanity as well as a symbol of excellence, and Carl Gustav Jung, whose God was similar to the God of the mystics—a psychological truth subjectively experienced by each individual.

It is interesting to note the similarities between Freud's three levels of personality and George Ivanovich Gurdjieff's idea of three common paths to enlightenment: the way of the fakir, or the man who masters his physical organism; the way of the monk, or the man who masters his emotions; and the way of the yogi, or the man who masters his mind. Gurdjieff believed there was a Fourth Way, though, which indicated that an ordinary man could reach enlightenment by practicing all three ways! Thus, enlightenment could be achieved through union of body, mind, and spirit, just as Freud suggested a highly developed personality could be achieved through balancing, understanding, and controlling the id, ego, and superego. Interestingly, Gurdjieff referred to his "system" as esoteric Christianity!

Western mystic and 11th-century philosopher St. Bonaventure wrote about the "three eyes" of humans, the three paths to gaining knowledge. The "eye of flesh" was the eye that sees the external, physical world of flesh. The "eye of reason" sees logic, philosophy, the realm of the mind. The "eye of contemplation" is the transcendent eye that gives a sense of oneness with the Cosmos. Again we see a reference to body, mind, and spirit.

Paganism and Triads

Even the earth religions of wicca and shamanism speak of a threefold nature or level of being to humanity. In *The Power of the Witch*, high priestess Laurie Cabot presents the life stages of a woman as maiden, mother, crone, which align with states of consciousness and knowingness. These stages, of innocence, knowledge, and wisdom, or birth, life, and death, are prevalent in the Hero's Journey myths we discussed earlier, proving you can't keep a good triadic concept of "natural being" down!

The shamans of the rainforests and the Siberian plains speak of three levels of existence and our ability to move between "Triple Worlds." Although they speak of them as physicalities, these levels, made up of the Lower World of man's subconscious nature; the Middle World of man's present physical reality; and the Upper World of union with higher beings, are also said to exist in the mind and can be accessed by altering one's state of consciousness.

The Welsh Triads

Some of the earliest triads are not of deities, but of sayings that depict the people, events, and locations that made up Medieval Britain. The number 3 heavily influenced a collection of three-line sayings called the Welsh Triads that suggest Celtic myth. One of the earliest collections of triads is found in the *Peniarth 16*, now housed at the National Library of Wales. Dating back to approximately the late 13th century, this and other similar manuscripts contain dozens of triads in the form of myths and stories. Many of the people mentioned in the triads are historical figures, and other figures of myth and legend. Some of these texts influenced Arthurian romance and may have actually been the origin point of Arthurian legend. Other important manuscripts include *Peniarth 45*, written about 1275 AD, the pair "White Book of Rhydderch" and "Red Book of Hergest," "The Mabinogion," "Lludd and Llefeys," "Peredur," and "Owain," and several of the stories in the Mabinogion feature Arthur himself, a man many scholars view as a more modern archetype of the "fisher king" or "priest-king," terms also ascribed to Christ. In many Arthurian legends, King Arthur is said to have 12 "best" knights seated at his famous Round Table, just as Christ had 12 apostles.

Whom Does the Trinity Serve?

So what did all this corresponding symbolism mean? If the Trinity was no longer believed to be a physical reality, but rather a symbol of

The Trinity Secret

something as profound as the nature of the divine itself, what was the symbol pointing to? Why was it so critical to the foundations of so many great spiritual traditions?

Like the mystical riddle of the Holy Grail, the question thus becomes: "Whom does the Trinity serve?"

A Sampling of Triple Deities Throughout History

Greek
Classical Greek triad of Zeus as Father, Leto as Mother, and Apollo as Son

Zeus, Athena, Apollo

Clotho, Lachesis, Atropos

Cerberus, a three-headed dog-like beast

Demeter, Dionysos, Kore

The Three Fates

The Three Furies

The Three Graces

The Gorgons

Triple Goddess Diana: Diana, Hecate, Nemorensis, also known as Persopene, Phoebe, Diana, and Hecate, Persephone, Selene

Roman
The Matrons or Three Mothers

Ceres, Liber Pater, Libera

Jupiter as Father, Juno as Mother, and Minerva as Daughter

The Three Fates and Furies (c orresponding to the Greek)

Egyptian
Osiris, Isis, Horus

Isis, Horus, Sub

Amun, Mut, Khonsu

Ptah, Sekhmet, Nefertem

Ra, Re-Horakty, Atum

Norse/Germanic/Celtic
The Norns

Odin, Vili, Ve

Triads, Triads, and More Triads

The Triglav
The Baltic Perkunas, Patrimpas, Pikoulis
The Auroras
Esus, Toutasis, Taranis
Brigit—Triple Goddess

Middle Eastern/Eastern

Three Daughters of Allah: al-Lat, Al-Uazza, Manat

The Saha Realm Trinity (Mahayana Buddhism)—Shakyamuni, Avalokitesvera, Ksitigarbha

Hindu mythology Brahma, Vishnu, Shiva (The Trimurti)

Hindu Mitra, Indra, Varune (Vedic)

Hindu Shakti, Lakshmi, Saraswati (Tridevi)

The Three Pure Ones of Taosim

Ayyavazhi Trinity

4

Archetype of Creation

Every natural fact is a symbol of some spiritual fact.
—Ralph Waldo Emerson

Every phenomenon of nature was a word, the sign, symbol and pledge of a new, mysterious, inexpressible but all the more intimate union, participation and community of divine energies and ideas.
—Johann G. Hamann

When we don't have the proper ability to describe something profound, we humans often turn to symbols and archetypes to illustrate that which cannot be put into words. Pictures, as they say, are worth a thousand words. The Trinity is no different. If the Trinity, as we suggest, symbolized more than just a specific description of one religious tradition's God, then why is it so often found in the symbolism and story of other cultures and traditions?

Ancient Sumerian cosmology centers on the "Enuma Elish," an epic poem of creation of the Gods and all other forms in existence. The *"Elish"* would later become a framework for many themes found in mystical Judaism and

Islam. The story begins with *Nammu*, the primeval sea and Mother of all, who created heaven (*an*) and Earth (*ki*). But when the hard metallic shell of the sky was separated and raised above earth by the God *Enlil*, there opened up a third layer of existence—that of the great waters of *Nammu*. Thus we have one of the first images of a triadic structure of existence on record. From this triadic primordial mess, the substance of which had been in existence for all eternity, the Gods themselves emerged two-by-two and the parade of creation began.

According to Gerald A. LaRue in *Ancient Myth and Modern Life*, this idea of a three-tiered structure found its way into ancient Greek, Egyptian, and even Hebrew creation myths, where heaven and earth were separated either by water (Egyptian) or air (Hebrew), or the Abyss of the Babylonian myth. These and other similar ancient creation myths would eventually develop into more symbolic descriptions of the universe, such as the shamanic belief in the Lower World, Middle World, and Upper World, and the much later Christian concept of heaven, hell, and purgatory.

Contemplating Creation

As ancient civilizations struggled to come to terms with the world around them, they began asking questions such as "Who or what created this? How was it created? Where do we stand in all of this?" These questions led to creation myths and stories that strived to explain great scientific concepts with minimal knowledge, and the symbolic and magical language that resulted tried nobly to "explain the inexplicable." Still, thinkers and philosophers alike wrestled with concepts with what little information they had available, and when they thought they had reasonably explained their physical existence, the natural progression toward spiritual understanding began.

Joseph Campbell spoke of this quest for spiritual knowledge in *The Power of Myth* when he wrote:

Around the end of the 12th Century, Abbot Joachim of Floris wrote of the three ages of Spirit. After the Fall of the Garden,

he said, God had to compensate for the disaster and reintroduce the spiritual principle into history. He chose a race to become the vehicle of this communication and that is the age of the Father and of Israel. And then this race, having been prepared as a priestly race, competent to become the vessel of incarnation, produces the Son.... The third age, which this philosopher in around 1260 said was now about to begin, is the age of the Holy Spirit, who speaks directly to the individual. Anyone who incarnates or brings into his life the message of the Word is equivalent to Jesus....

Suddenly, humans were far less concerned with figuring out the physical makeup of the Universe, and much more concerned about the spiritual makeup of their own being. Heaven became a symbol for God, or the Ultimate Divine. The Earth was the realm of the Son, or Jesus, and those striving toward Divine Union. In between was the magical realm of the Holy Spirit, where a normal man or woman could reach enlightenment or contact with God.

Campbell suggested that behind all concepts of duality (that is, man/woman, man/divine, good/evil, light/dark, heaven/earth) lies an even greater singularity of truth that unites the two into one whole: "I and you, this and that, true and untrue—every one of them has its opposite. But mythology suggests that behind that duality there is a singularity over which this plays like a shadow game." This singularity is later described as a concept of transcendence, not unlike the Holy Spirit as the unifying glue between two opposites, Father and Son (Divine and Human). But, as we suggest, it may also describe a concept of process, or activity, which manifests the human from the divine.

Campbell also suggested that the Trinity Concept may have always been present, but grew stronger as a spiritual idea with the rise of patriarchal religions. Earlier Goddess-based religions suggested that the whole of entirety was within the body of the Great Mother, but in patriarchal religions God is seen as a separate entity far from human reach, thus the greater need for a spiritual idea of how to reach that far-off God.

Archetype of Creation

Ancient paganism and shamanism suggest that even within the realm of a genderless divinity there were still three levels of existence humans would be forced to contend with: the physical, mental, and spiritual, or more easily termed as body, mind, and spirit. Even Neoplatonists understood this basic Hermetic Law: As Above, So Below. Earth-based religions understood the connection between man, nature, and the creative force behind it all. Shamans journeyed through the vast realms of the Lower World, where the most base primal existence occurred; the Middle World of day-to-day existence; and the Upper World, where superior guidance and knowledge was available. At least 40,000 years before the dawn of Christianity, shamanic peoples understood that the only way to wholeness and connection with the creative force was to be able to move easily between the Triple Worlds, and to be able to transcend the limits of the body and mind in order to enter the realm of pure spirit.

Precursors of Later Trinity Symbolism

Were these ideas precursors of later concepts of God, man, and Holy Spirit? Perhaps even precursors of the much later concepts of id, ego, and superego as introduced by Freud and later reconstructed to indicate the subconscious, conscious, and superconscious? And what about the Buddhist concept of Personhood, Mindfulness, and Nirvana? Or the Metaphysical suggestion of Self, Conscious Awareness, and Higher Self? And the much more recent concept of Right Brain/Intuitive, Left Brain/Analytical, and Third Eye/Spiritual?

The ancient myths and stories of creation, including the Egyptian tale of the Reigning Queen as Mother of God, the Reigning Pharaoh as Sun God or Father immanent in the flesh among men, and the Heir Apparent (Prince) as the Son both of God and God to be, all speak of a triadic structure upon which humans could understand not only the way the world around them was made, but the way they themselves were made and meant to express their being. This idea of expression would repeat itself throughout history, from Queen, Pharaoh, and Prince/Son; to Buddha, Dharma, and Sangha; to God, Christ, and Adam; to Father,

Son, and Holy Spirit; to today's popular notion of Me, Myself, and I. And as humankind continued to struggle with the need to understand his world, both outer and inner, this triadic concept would find expression in every aspect of his nature—physical, psychological, and spiritual.

To understand the parallels between Trinity Concepts from ancient times to present day, one must only line them up to see that they all speak of both a reality and a process that describes the path to union with God, or the Divine. Often, the Trinity is seen as a powerful symbol, as in the archetypes of the unconscious made famous by Carl Jung. But what is most interesting is the way each culture and historical age chooses to interpret the identical concept, whether it be reality, symbol, or process. One could then say that the Trinity Concept itself had a triadic nature all its own.

Thus arises the need to present the Trinity interpretations in three separate sections, beginning with the physical.

The Emergence of Trinity Imagery

Ancient civilizations lacked the cutting-edge technology of today, and thus viewed their world through the eyes of magic and awesome wonder. Thus, the birth of the triadic nature of being emanated from the actual stories of creation of the physical world, the coming together of land, sea, and air to create a unified earth.

Physical "Trinities" are most present in such creation myths, long before the dawn of civilization and the introduction of basic sciences such as astronomy, mathematics, and geography that evolved during ancient Sumeria and through the progressive history of the Mesopotamian region. Before anybody had any idea that there was such a thing as science, there were only the heavens above, the earth below, and the waters that separated the two and punctuated the far horizon. As humans evolved inward, this imagery, too, turned inward, and humans began contemplating their physical makeup: Am I body? Am I this thing that thinks? Am I this spirit moving within the deepest parts of me? Or am I all three of these combined into one?

Archetype of Creation

Thus began the move away from the Trinity as a physical entity and toward a more inward, symbolic interpretation that may have paralleled the physical world, but went far beyond the limitations of physicality.

The Trinity of ancient Egypt joined the powerful Mother of God as Queen with the Father God element of Pharaoh to create the Son of God, or the Prince that would walk among the people. Although these were actual entities, even the Egyptians believed that they could experience the same wholeness of Divine Union—the uniting of the three symbols within themselves. LaRue reminds us that ancient Egyptian hymns often speak of an all-pervading joy experienced when the worshippers experience moments of divine-human union, as if a holy breath of spirit (Holy Spirit) suddenly awakened them to the beauty and joy of life. An ancient Egyptian could worship the entity of the Trinity in the form of an actual Queen with her Pharaoh and their son, the Prince, yet also know that he himself was made of that same triadic nature. Therefore, the physical becomes the spiritual, so to speak.

According to the Babylonians, all Gods were grouped into triads, including the main figure of Mithras, who was alleged to have a secret triadic nature. Earlier Semitic Gods came in triads as well. Baal of Edessa (Sun) was accompanied by Aziz (Mars) and Monimos (Mercury). Mercury would eventually become Hermes, and, during the Middle Ages, Hermes would be renamed Hermes Trismegistus, Triple Wise One!

Tribal shamans around the world viewed their Universe as a three-tiered "Triple World." This corresponds with the ancient Chinese cosmology of "heaven/man/earth," which was also a physical reality to the Chinese, who believed one must be able to move between all levels to achieve insight and enlightenment.

Both the ancient Chinese and shamans believed that there must be a balance between the worlds of spirit, of nature, and of man in order to end suffering, and that the human realm could not survive without either the spirit or natural world intact and healthy. They treated these realms as actual realities, applicable to both their outer world and their inner world.

Goddess-based religions suggest an entity-based triad of Maiden, Mother, Crone. These were not only actual physical entities present in each woman's life, but actual growth stages each woman went through between birth, life, and death. The Maiden symbolized the young woman of nubile, marrying age. The Mother was the woman that nurtured her child and gave birth to new life. The Crone was the wise older woman in each family, the ancient grandmother full of wisdom and experience. And although each woman knew the Maiden, Mother, and Crone in her own family and circle of friends, she was also the triad itself (even if she chose to be childless, for Mothers could give birth to creativity other than little children!). This symbolism was often associated with the moon and its three phases of new, waxing/waning, and full.

Fig. 4-1

Fig. 4-2

These two images represent the triune nature in paganism and modern witchcraft. Again, these are archetypal symbols that use images to convey the profound nature of the triple-Goddess in all her phases.

According to Carl Jung, even Neoplatonist Plotinus described a threefold physical world nature: Uranos as the Transcendent One, Kronos as the Son, and Zeus as the world-soul subordinate to the Son. Plotinus describes the One as hypostatic, thus being the underlying essence of the three, a theory later supported by the Nicaean Council of Christian Bishops and of Constantinople in AD 325 in their respective struggles to define the Trinity.

The Hindu Rig Veda tells of the manifestation of the Divine as a "*trimurti*" or triad of deities made up of Brahma, the power of creation; Vishnu in 10 incarnations, the power of preservation; and Shiva,

Archetype of Creation

the power of destruction. These physical deities also could be found within humankind, as the source of inner creativity, preservation, and destruction. The Hindus, as did most ancient Eastern and Western traditions, believed in the Hermetic Law of "As Above, So Below." What appeared to be occurring in the realm of the Gods and Goddesses, also seemed to be occurring within man himself.

BRAHMA   VISHNU   SHIVA

Fig. 4-3

The Hindu Trimurti of Brahma, Vishnu and Shiva.

Still, the most obvious physical Trinity occurs in Christianity, where the Father, Son, and Holy Spirit are first described as actual beings. The Father is God, the Son is the Christ, also called Son of God and Son of Man, and the Holy Spirit is often described in the New Testament as a "presence which descended upon" whomever was the lucky chosen. But even the Christian church in its earliest configuration had issues with the simplistic, physical-oriented Trinity. If Jesus was the Son, yet also the Word (*Logos*) made flesh, was he, too, God? Was the Christ made of the same nature as God? And who or what was the Holy Spirit?

Let us reiterate that when the early church bishops gathered at the Council of Nicaea in the year AD 325, they actually resolved (although there were a few dissenters) this questioning by creating the Apostles'

The Trinity Secret

Creed, which would from that point on state that the Creator and the Redeemer were one and the same. At this point, the Trinity became less a physical reality and more a spiritual symbol and a path to divine union, with God as the Father Almighty, the Son of God as Lord Jesus Christ, and the Holy Spirit as the binding agent, so to speak, between the two (more on the nature of the Holy Spirit later).

Yet even as Christianity developed, and as Gnostic and Mystical Christianity began to grow, the somewhat physical concept of One God, One Son (Jesus) and some mysterious third "entity" as Holy Spirit began to expand into something more symbolic and less material. This was part of the natural evolution of human thought and spiritual unfoldment. Most of the original concepts of a Trinity began just as human thought began: simplistic, physical-oriented, based upon what could be seen and immediately understood within the physical and material realm. But the more man developed, and the more his consciousness expanded, the farther away from a physical nature the Trinity Concept moved.

From Physical to Symbolic

Before we can examine the Trinity as a process, we must first see how the concept itself evolved from a purely physical nature into something more symbolic. The term *archetype*, made famous by Carl Jung, describes a model or example by which all other things are made, or prototype. For Jung, the archetypes of the collective unconscious describe powerful symbols of being and experience that are common to all humankind. In philosophy, archetypes refer to ideal forms of the perceived or sensible things or types. The origins of the archetypal hypothesis seem to date back to the philosopher Plato. Platonic ideas heavily influenced the later work of Jung. Plato's ideas, according to Wikipedia, "were pure mental forms imprinted in the soul before it was born into the world. They were collective in the sense that they embodied the fundamental characteristics of a thing rather than its specific peculiarities."

Jung described *archetype* in A Psychological Approach to the Dogma of the Trinity:

Archetype of Creation

have often been asked where the archetype comes from and whether it is acquired or not. This question cannot be answered directly. Archetypes are, by definition, factors and motifs that arrange the psychic elements into certain images, characterized as archetypal, but in such a way that they can be recognized only from the effects they produce. They exist preconsciously, and presumably they form the structural dominants of the psyche in general. They may be compared to the invisible presence of the crystal lattice in a saturated solution. As a priori conditioning factors they represent a special, psychological instance of the biological "pattern of behaviour," which gives all living organisms their specific qualities. Just as the manifestations of this biological ground plan may change in the course of development, so also can those of the archetype. Empirically considered, however, the archetype did not ever come into existence as a phenomenon of organic life, but entered into the picture with life itself.

Archetypes serve to offer a more basic, fundamental function of understanding that work deeply in the level of the unconscious. According to Adam Blatner, MD, in *The Relevance of the Concept of 'Archetype*, "Archetypes are the extensions of the phenomenon of instinct, as complexified and expressed in human experience. In themselves formless and expressing the sociobiological dimension of neurophysiology, their manifestations may be found in themes of art, ritual, custom, imagery, dreams, philosophy, psychopathology, and every other human endeavor." The archetype is the domain of the unconscious, where perceptions and ideas lurk that have not made it to the level of conscious awareness.

According to Barbara F. McManus, professor of Classics Emerita at the College of New Rochelle, archetypes consist of three elements:

- ❧ They carry a high emotional charge (positive, negative, or both simultaneously); they have a powerful, compelling effect.

- ❧ For an individual, they frequently recur in situations when the rational, conscious mind is not in full control (e.g., recurring dreams and fantasies, obsessive behavior patterns that have no fully rational explanation).

❀ This recurrence occurs also in many different eras and cultures (e.g., commonly used symbols in literature, art, and life; recurring types of dreams; mythic patterns, etc.).

McManus writes in *The Jungian Approach to Symbolic Interpretaion* that archetypes constitute a theory to explain the constant recurrence, persistence, and emotional power of certain ways of symbolizing reality:

Their manifestations (a rchetypal images) are always personally and culturally conditioned. In given individuals and cultures, some archetypes are activated and others dormant; we say that their 'triggers' are based on personal and cultural experience, though the archetypes are universal. A study of archetypal symbolism in myth provides us with maps, not dictionaries.

Jung recognized that many of these universal images are based upon universal emotions such as fear, desire, joy, and awe. These images—these archetypes—are found everywhere in many forms, such as heroes and demons, good and evil parents, even Gods, magicians, and monsters. McManus states that the universality of these images occurs in every human being, and, are hard-wired into us emotionally and relate to our perceptions of a particular world we are experiencing.

Instinct is not as simple as we often think it is. It goes beyond our "natural reactions" to our environment, or our primitive drives, fears, and beliefs. Instinct goes beyond the level of mere survival tools to, as Blatner describes, "themes of territoriality, dominance, group hunting," and these instincts take on a sort of "human form" in the layer of the unconscious in which they are found. He goes on to state that consciousness, human consciousness, has transformed instinct into archetype, which are "tendencies rather than forms" the "intrinsic pattern" rather then the "clothing of the pattern" itself. Thus the archetype has the role of describing a special experience that cannot be easily explained or described in words, or other theoretical models,

Archetype of Creation

such as the experience of oneness with God, agape love, and the more magical feelings of "numinosity," including near-death experiences and ecstatic religious visions. You simply cannot describe these mysteries in simple words and phrases. They are experienced in a deeper level, and therefore require a deeper level of expression.

Even numbers can be seen as archetypes, especially primary numbers. If 2 represents duality, then 3 is the unification of duality, a completeness, a wholeness. The black-or-white thinking of the common mind could find a deeper sense of truth in the unifying principle of a Trinity. Thus a triad would signify two dual natures, and the synthesizing element that includes the other two. Blatner suggests perhaps Christ was the mediator or synthesizer between God, the creative force, and man, but in fact, that role would be played by the Holy Spirit, as we propose. Between the divine and the human, there is the quality of synthesis that makes one possible out of the other.

Sacred Archetypes of the Trinity

Long before Jung, the Holy Trinity was taking shape as the perfect archetype of man's divine inner nature. In ancient Chinese cosmology, the sacred triad of heaven, earth, and man considered man as the link between the two, later paralleled in the sacred ternary of Deus (God), Homo (Man), and Natura (Nature) in medieval Western Tradition. These reality-based concepts eventually added on a spiritual or inner-directed context as humankind began to journey inward to answer the questions surrounding existence and being.

We also see this triune nature unfolding into a non-reality concept of inner awareness in Siberian and South American shamanism, with the Triple Worlds representing not just the actual levels of the Universe they could journey between, but levels of the human consciousness they could journey between as well.

The driving force for man to be both at one with nature and with God had created the need to at first unite the inner forces of primal instinct, everyday consciousness, and supreme enlightenment. Individually and collectively, humankind sought to unite the body, mind, and spirit through symbols and stories. The concept of the Trinity was the most powerful of these symbols.

Again we turn to Joseph Campbell, who discusses the commonalities he found in all ancient mythologies and their stories of the Hero's Journey, by which an ordinary mortal (Son) went through a powerful initiation/journey (Holy Spirit) and was transformed (Father). This Hero archetype played a powerful part in all the great stories and legends, including the epic Gilgamesh tale, of a triadic experience of separation, initiation, and return. We see this archetype today in the *Star Wars* stories, where Luke Skywalker sets out on a challenge-filled journey to save his planet and other worlds from the evil Darth Vader and his sinister cohorts. Luke undergoes a trial by fire of sorts, becoming transformed and gaining knowledge that empowers and changes him in the most profound ways. The Hero's actual journey itself has even become an archetype of sorts, and the Trinity Concept closely parallels the journey's threefold nature, as we shall see later when we discuss processes of enlightenment.

Another startling example of a symbolic Trinity occurs when we look at what Campbell refers to as the Freudian (and, later, Jungian) concept of the infant in relation to its father and mother, a concept played out in paintings and drawings of Homo sapiens cave art some 40,000 years ago. Images of men on these cave walls were always clothed, yet females were always portrayed as naked in their glory, suggesting that the mother represented the power of nature, and the father that of societal authority, thus producing a child who would be a combination of the two and be raised as such.

This and other similar thoughts would be echoed in the ancient Eastern wisdom schools as well. In his introduction to Barbara Stoler Miller's translation, *The Bhagavad-Gita*, Huston Smith states, "To uncover the nature of the self, the Gita approaches it from three directions that triangulate the self…. One of these concerns its makeup, its attributes or qualities. A second distinguishes different spiritual attitudes that serve as starting points for the journey to God…the third system of classification turns on differences in what grabs people's interests in the world." All three attributes, per Smith, create a model of the human self and his psychological and spiritual nature.

Archetype of Creation

Even the various aspects of Krishna's material nature are described as Triadic and are analyzed in terms of the three fundamental qualities of lucidity (*sattva*), passion (*rajas*), and dark inertia (*tamas*). These three natural qualities are what constitute, in Hindu thought, the nature of man.

Three Levels of Heaven, Hell, and Earth

We are being told here that the higher self resides in the upper realms of the world, of reality, of consciousness. Men caught in the in-between are stuck to their passions, unable to rise above them and find true heaven. Those who give in to dark inertia sink into the bowels of hell, where their flesh-driven ways annihilate any opportunity for growth and enlightenment. This process symbolizes the choices we have as humans both in a physical and a spiritual sense. Heaven may simply be the archetype of enlightenment; purgatory, the archetype of indifference; Hell, the archetype of the primal drives of humanness. One is reached via lucidity or the clearness of thought and the ability to perceive truth. One is reached by simply going along with the passions and emotions of being human, with no desire to rise above the fray of living entirely from the five senses, without connection to a higher level of understanding. The last of course is reached by giving in to temptations of greed, lust, gluttony, and the baser qualities of man.

This tri-level concept of heaven is mirrored in the doctrines of Joseph Smith, founder of the Church of Jesus Christ and the Latter Day Saints (LDS, or Mormons). In Smith's translation of the Book of Mormon, he introduced his belief that heaven has more than one "kingdom." He identifies three levels of heaven, or levels of glory, that are described in detail in the Doctrine and Covenants. The levels are: the celestial, the level of the glory of the sun, the glory of God, the highest level of all; the terrestrial, the level of "the church of the Firstborn who have received the fullness of the Father," the earth-bound believers; and the lowest level of all, the telestial, which is basically hell for those who do not believe in the gospel and teachings of Christ (the Mormon version).

In the New Testament, Paul speaks of a "third heaven" in his second letter to the Corinthians (2 Cor. 12:2), which would be the home of God, the highest heaven.

The Trinity archetype of a threefold creation allows for many descriptions and illustrations of this ongoing quest to achieve higher wisdom, growth, and knowledge. One must always start at the bottom, spend some time in the middle, and eventually, one hopes in this lifetime, reach the top in order to view the wholeness of creation from the highest vantage point. This process of growth is, in itself, a process of creation—the creation of a sage, an enlightened being, one who, according to some doctrines, will not have to come back and do it all over again.

The concept of creation is also evident as symbol in Father-Mother-Child. The Father represents the giving seed, the transmitter of life. The Mother is the receiver of the seed who nurtures the seed into a full life form through her own body. The Child is their creation, the new seed that will one day repeat this very same process. That is the chain of life. Birth, life, death. Followed by a new opportunity for birth, life, and death again.

Even the double Trinity takes on importance, most notably in the Yahwist symbol of the Star of David, which Jung believed was an unconscious recognition of the Trinity.

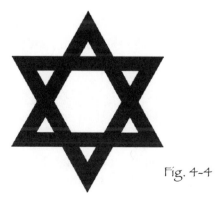

Fig. 4-4

The Star of David.

Archetype of Creation

Variations of 3

The number 6, 3 doubled, was thought to embody both male and female forces, and is also served to symbolize opposites united as one. In *The Living Symbol*, Gerhard Adler, a Jung disciple, explores the female and male triads as having different roles. The female triad is associated with "instinctual events"; the male triad is about the concept of thesis, antithesis, and reconciliation of the two. Jung would adopt the quaternity eventually as being more representative of these dual forces, but even he admitted in *The Archetypes and the Collective Unconscious* that the quaternity is imagined as a square divided into two halves by a diagonal, the end result being two triangles with apices pointing in opposing directions. Thus, metaphorically, this four-square or quaternity encompasses the two opposing triads. Critics would later say that Jung's entire works were in truth based upon the number 6, or the double triad number, instead of the number 4 or even 3. Such confusion over archetypes continues to this day, with negative connotations placed upon the number 666, and the most evil of numbers in Christiandom (although a lucky number for the Chinese!).

Plato also recognized this division of the quaternity, the square, which led to his view of the whole of existence as being based upon the triangular form. He divided the soul into spirit, desire, and reason, and incorporated this into many of his works. Jung's focus on the quaternity also focused on more psychological aspects of the mind, symbolizing "psychic wholeness," and often viewed Trinitarian symbolism as incomplete. But he did recognize the power of the Trinity as the unifying force of two sides, something only a threefold nature could suggest.

The Three Lights of Paracelsus

Paracelsus (born Phillippus Aureolus Theophrastus Bombastus von Hohenheim, 1493–1541), the great philosopher, alchemist, and Theosophist, who had a considerable influence on the hermetic philosophers of the 16th and 17th centuries, wrote of "the three lights" in his *Astronomia Magna*, a treatise on the microcosm and macrocosm (As

Above, So Below). These three lights were: the elemental, or material, body; the sidereal, or ethereal body; and the eternal, or luminous body. Paracelsus instructed man to study in all three schools to truly know thyself: "For three lights burn in man, and accordingly three doctrines are prescribed to him. Only all three together make man perfect. Although the first two lights shine but dimly in comparison with the brilliant third light, they too are lights of the world and man must walk his earthly path in their radiance." The material, the sidereal, and the eternal.

According to the teachings of Theosophy, Paracelsus stressed the Unity of Nature underlying everything in existence as a whole as well as the inter-relationship and interdependence of all its parts: "Nature, being the Universe, is ONE, and its origin can only be the one eternal Unity. It is an organism in which all things harmonize and sympathize with each other. It is the Macrocosm. Man is the Microcosm. And the Macrocosm and Microcosm are ONE. (*Philosophia ad Athenienses*.)"

This unity of man and Nature makes man the focal point through which the three worlds of Nature—the physical, astral, and spiritual—manifest themselves. These three "worlds" are made up of a vast quantity of "beings" or "lives." Some of the "lives" are intelligent, others unintelligent, and it is man's duty to understand their nature. The ignorant man may be controlled by the lower lives. But the true philosopher has learned how to control them by the power of the Supreme Creator within himself.

Man's first task, therefore, is to *know himself*. He must become acquainted with the complexities of his own nature, but, in pursuing this study, he must never for a moment separate himself from Great Nature, of which he is a copy and a part. "Try to understand yourselves in the light of Nature," he advised his students, "and then all wisdom will come to you."

In the I Ching, we find that humans are linked with both the heavens and the earth, the realms of ideas and of material things, forming a Trinity so primal it is an archetype everyone understands on a deep, instinctual level. Even the T'ai Hsuan Ching, similar to the I Ching, focuses on the Trinity of heaven, earth, and man as primordial. Yet, the

Trinity archetype might also suggest something entirely inward, as in the works of Dr. F.C. Happold. In his *Mysticism*, he describes three types of mysticism: nature-mysticism, soul-mysticism, and God-mysticism. This universal concept of an internal Trinity is also mirrored in the works of English historian Arnold Toynbee, who states in *An Historian's Approach to Religion* that despite the variety of religious practices, one quest remains clear in all of them—the three objectives of Nature, Man, and an Absolute Reality that is "no either nature or Man but is in them and at the same time beyond them."

Again, in the writings of Joseph Campbell, the myths offer ample evidence of an archetypal test consisting of three attempts, all of which the hero must overcome to achieve his or her goal. Campbell also wrote about the life force itself being made of three components: the physical circulation of food substance, the dynamic stream of energy, and the spiritual manifestation of Grace.

In the next chapter we will go one step further and examine how the Trinity has gone from being an archetype of the subconscious to an intrinsic part of our language, our folklore, and our way of telling the stories that impart the wisdom, knowledge, and lessons of humanity. Notice all the threes in that last sentence? There truly is a reason why there were three little pigs, and not four.

The Trinity Secret

5

The Power of
the Three

Three is the mystery, come from the great one.
Hear, and light on thee will dawn.
—The Emerald Tablets of Thoth the Atlantean

Three things cannot be long hidden: the sun, the moon, and the truth.
—Gautama Siddhartha

All things that are specifically complete are stamped with this
number 3.
—E.W. Bullinger

Birth, life, death. Body, mind, spirit. Past, present, future. Height, width, depth. Sky, earth, sea. Moe, Larry, Curly.

You get the drift. For some reason, which we will explore fully in this chapter, things often come in threes. In the Appendix, we present an extensive list of famous "threes," but for now, suffice it to say, they are everywhere. If you look hard enough, you can find evidence of the importance of any number. But for 3, you don't have to look that hard. It is present both in a physical sense, as well as a non-physical sense. Let's start with the physical.

Three is a prime number, a Fibonacci number, a Lucas number. Three has its own branch of mathematics called trigonometry, which is based on measuring triangles. Triangles can be broken down into acute, right, and obtuse angles. We live in a world of three dimensions (spatial), and we measure yards by 3 feet and leagues by 3 miles. We measure time by seconds, minutes, and hours, and we define our lives according to past, present, and future events and experiences.

There are three primary colors by which we create all others, and three types of cones in the backs of our eyes that are made to pick up on different wavelengths of light. In the world of art, there are three color levels on the color wheel: primary, secondary, and tertiary.

Many medical conditions are diagnosed according to three signs or symptoms, including Beck's triad for cardiology, Cushing's triad for head injuries, and MacDonald's triad for personality disorder/antisocial behavior.

We give three cheers—"Hip Hip Hooray"—and we use three steps of reasoning: thesis, antithesis, and synthesis. We were told we have three unalienable rights: life, liberty, and the pursuit of happiness. But that is often up to the government, which is made up of the executive, legislative, and judicial branches. Maybe only as long as we "see no evil, hear no evil, and speak no evil." By the way, those three monkeys that make up the Three Wise Monkey philosophy of the Japanese had actual names: Kikazaru covered his ears to hear no evil, Iwazaru covered his mouth to speak no evil, and Mizaru covered his eyes to see no evil. Who knew?

Heck, we even live on the third rock from the sun!

Fig. 5-1

The evolution of the number 3 from Brahmin Indians to Europeans.

Please Allow Me to Introduce Myself—I Am Three

3 is the first prime number—a natural number that has exactly two distinct natural number divisors: 1 and itself.

3 is a Lucas number—a number in an integer sequence named after the mathematician Francois Edouard Anatole Lucas (1842–1891), defined to be the sum of its two immediate previous terms; in other words, it is a Fibonacci integer sequence. Consequently, the ratio between two consecutive Lucas numbers converges to the golden ratio.

3 is a Fibonacci number—named after Leonardo of Pisa; each subsequent number is the sum of the previous two.

3 is a Mersenne number—named after Marin Mersenne; a positive integer that is one less than a power of two.

3 is a Triangular number—the number of dots in an equilateral triangle evenly filled with dots.

3 is a Cullen number—no relation to the *Twilight* vampire series. A Cullen number is a natural number of the form $n-2 n$ (1 written Cn). Cullen numbers were first studied by Fr. James Cullen in 1905. Almost all Cullen numbers are composite, and none of them suck blood.

3 is a Super Catalan number—Catalan numbers are the number of p good paths from to (6 0,0) that do not cross the diagonal line. Super Catalan numbers count the number of lattice paths with diagonal steps from to (0 ,0) which do not touch the diagonal line. (Huh?)

And all this time, you thought 3 was just one more than 2.

If I am rubber, and you are glue, then for some strange reason, it is widely believed that whatever you say to me comes back to you— threefold. The only things you need to survive are breathing, drinking, and eating (we will leave sex out of this for now!). If you get up early, you will be healthy, wealthy, and wise (and catch the worm to boot). And you can use weight, number, and measure to decide just how

The Power of the Three

healthy, wealthy, and wise you really are. In fact, without 3, you have nothing. Think about it. All closed and complete geometric forms have a minimum of three lines. Two lines won't cut it.

And if every Tom, Dick, and Harry were tall, dark, and handsome, women would be ready, willing, and able to stop, look, and listen to what they had to say!

If you want to run a race, wait for the count: "On your mark…one…two…three!" On the count of three, you can get people to do things in unison. Three is lucky in Cantonese because it sounds like the word for "alive," as opposed to 4, which sounds like the word for "death." In Vietnamese culture, it is bad luck to take a photo with three people in it because the person in the middle is said to die soon afterward. If you travel to Vietnam, don't stand in the middle of any photo ops! The third time is always the charm, although not for celebrities. Celebrities seem to die in threes (although this is based upon society's idea of celebrity), and good things come in threes (are we just ignoring the stuff that comes before and after?) And have you ever opened a pod of peas and actually found three peas in a pod? Hopefully so. Many of you reading this are once, twice, three times a lady. And if you are a self-involved lady, you really only care about me, myself, and I. One is the loneliest number, and apparently, two can be as sad as one, according to a popular rock band from the '60s and '70s.

Three strikes and you're out, but you can always go and row-row-row your boat while holding your three-ring binder that contains your school report on the *Nina*, the *Pinta*, and the *Santa Maria*. Are you rich, poor, or middle class? Happy, sad, or indifferent? Alive, dead, or zombie? Okay, that last one was just plain reaching!

There are RNA, DNA, and proteins, and persons, places, and things. We just love to group things into threes, and find groups of three that already exist.

Legend and lore from the first World War states that you should never be the third person to light a cigarette in a group. Why? Seems during wartime, in the trenches, the enemy would see the first light, aim for the second, and fire upon the third. Moms and dads worldwide use the count of 3 to threaten punishment. "If I have to count to 3, I'll…" though few parents ever really follow through.

The basis of a musical chord is a triad of three notes. And you cannot have a trio without three players. Somebody has to hold up that big bass!

Even the Family of Man is divided into three parts according to a recent analysis of the genomes of 53 human populations. The end result of the studies leading to this analysis state that there are only three genetic groups that make up the all of humanity. According to studies conducted by Jonathan K. Pritchard for the University of Chicago, and featured in the June 2009 volume of the online journal *PLoS Genetics*, these groups are directly linked to the first "walk out of Africa" about 70,000 years ago, when a small group of Homo sapiens made the most important trek of mankind. The three groups are African, which contains descendants of original humans who emerged 200,000 years ago in East Africa; Eurasians, which include the natives of Europe, the Middle East, and Southwest Asia; and the East Asian, which encompasses the peoples of Asia, Japan, and Southeast Asia, and because of the existence of the Bering Land Bridge and island-to-island travel in the South Pacific, this group includes the inhabitants of the Americas as well.

By the way, the surface of the Earth is one-third land and two-thirds water. At any point on earth you can gaze up at the sun, stars, and moon that make up our heavenly corner of the universe.

There are three forms of matter: solid, liquid, and gas, and before we learned about the world of microbes, we once defined nature in three kingdoms: animal, vegetable, and mineral. Thought, word, and deed make up the sum of human capability.

In the Buddhist Wheel of Life, there are Three Cardinal Faults of humans: greed, hatred, and delusion, represented by the pig, snake, and cock. In Shinto, there are three symbols of the sun Goddess: The Mirror, truth and wisdom; the Jewel, compassion; and the Sword, courage and strength. For some reason, poor Jonah had to spend three days and three nights in the belly of a whale to learn his lessons. Three people passed by a half-dead man they could have helped. The first two, the priest and Levite, walked by. The third was a Samaritan, who did stop to help, and thus Auto Club was born.

The Power of the Three

Be careful what you wish for, because the Genii only promised three wishes. Although many of us would love to have a Close Encounter of the Third Kind. And we all know what happened at Three Mile Island....

All in good fun, we say, and are certain that you could take any number and find all kinds of significant connections, but not like the number 3.

The Mighty Number 3

In the past chapters we've looked at the Trinity Concept, where it came from, and how other cultures and traditions had their own "triune" take on the world they inhabited. Now it's all about the number itself. Three. 3.

The number has become sacred, more so than any other, and there are reasons why, which we shall explore in the next few chapters. Why did this particular number become held in such high regard, throughout history, especially in our belief systems and religious traditions, which often shape our understanding of who we are and why we are here?

So many times in the big three Western traditions of Christianity, Judaism, and Islam, the number pops up, suggesting a more mystical significance than might appear on the surface. Other numbers do indeed also play important roles, but 3 reigns supreme, and maybe that is why. Three is the number of unity, which unites dual or opposing forces. Three is the number of completion, wholeness, allness. Even the number 1 cannot compare, even though it should alone represent allness. After all, all is one, isn't it? But apparently, in the minds of sages, philosophers, and master teachers alike, three is all, three is one, and 3 is the number to be revered above all others.

It is the number of multiplicity, and the number of synthesis.

We found a wonderful quote on the Website Greatdreams.com that sums up the importance of the number 3: "In the first three numbers, all of the others are synthesized. From the union of oneness and duality (which is its reflection), that is, from triad, proceed all of the other numbers, and from this primordial triangle all figures derive."

Judeo-Christians find many interesting references to the number 3 in the Old and New Testaments:

- ✻ Three angels visit Abraham to announce that his wife, Sarah, will give birth to a son.

- ✻ Noah had three sons: Shem, Ham, and Japeth.

- ✻ Joseph imprisoned his brothers for three days when they arrived in Egypt.

- ✻ Jonah spent three days and three nights in the belly of a whale.

- ✻ Just as Jonah spent three days and three nights in the whale's belly, we are told in Matthew 12:40 that "so will the Son of Man be three days and three nights in the heart of the earth...."

- ✻ Three Wise Men bearing three gifts followed the Star of Bethlehem to the site of the holy birth of Christ.

- ✻ Satan attempted to tempt Jesus in the desert three times.

- ✻ Jesus spoke of a threefold rule: "I am the way, and the truth, and the life...."

- ✻ Jesus spread the Christian word for three years.

- ✻ Jesus predicted that Peter would deny him three times.

- ✻ Jesus died at the age of 33.

- ✻ Jesus rose from the dead on the third day.

- ✻ Jesus appeared three times after his death.

- ✻ Jesus raised three persons from the dead.

- ✻ There were three crosses at Calvary.

- ✻ There were three Marys.

- ✻ There are three graces or virtues referred to in 1 Corinthians 13: faith, hope, and charity.

- ✻ There were three natures to temptation: the lust of the flesh, the lust of the eyes, and the pride of life, according to 1 John 2:16.

The Power of the Three

- Man was threefold in nature, as body, soul and spirit.

- There were three patriarchs of Judaism: Abraham, Isaac, and Jacob.

- The Tanakh has three sections: Torah, Nevl'lm, and Ketuvim.

- The Torah was given in the third month of the Jewish year, to the three groups or main divisions of Jews—Kohen, Levi, and Israel.

- The Torah was given through Moses, the third child in his family, and was given in three portions: the Five Books of Moses, the Prophets, and the Writings.

- In Hebrew philosophy the world stands on three things: Torah, prayer, and acts of kindness. The world exists because of justice, truth, and peace.

- Muslims repeat certain devotional rites three times, others 33.

- Muslims make pilgrimage to three holy cities: Mecca, Medina, and Jerusalem.

- There are three mitzvos of the seder: the lamb, matzah, and maror.

- There are three means by which to gain atonement: teshuvah, repentance; tefillah, prayer; and tzadakah, charity.

- In Kabbalistic thought, there are three aspects of the soul in the Zohar's teachings: nefesh, life force; ruach, unseen mind; and the spiritual aspect of neshamah.

- To Kabbalists, 3 is the number of integration.

This list is in no way complete, but gives a good picture of the prevalence and presence of the number 3 in Western religious thought. But why?

The idea that doing something not once, or twice, but three times seems to add an aspect of strength and power to what we do. One may symbolize unity and peace, with nothing to affect or disturb it.

The Trinity Secret

Two presents the challenge and tension of duality, of an opposing force. Three unifies and brings balance, equilibrium, and harmony. Three not only stands alone as three, but also as encompassing the two opposites it has unified. That is the meaning behind reverent marriage vows that two shall become as one yet united there will be three: each person in the marriage, and the whole of the relationship between them.

To those practicing Western religious traditions, 3 is the number of divine perfection, and divine completion. Beginning, middle, and end. God's own attributes are threefold: omniscience, omnipresence, and omnipotence. Many prayers and devotions must be repeated three times to ensure their purpose. We as humans might also, on a deeper subconscious level, recognize that we have three ways of being in the world: in relationship to oneself, in relationship to others, and in relationship to God, or to nature if one does not believe in a deity.

Even the Freemasons revered the number 3. In *The Encyclopedia of Freemasonry* we are told, "Everywhere among the ancients, the number three was deemed the most sacred of numbers." The Masons refer to the ancient Chinese belief that numbers reach perfection at 3, which then "denotes the multiplicity of any object by repeating the character which stands for it three times." They even throw props to Plato and Aristotle for recognizing that the number is the image of the Supreme Being itself, because it contains all properties of dualities. It is beginning, middle, and end, or, as Pythagoras once stated, the number of perfect harmony.

Freemasonry has 33 degrees by which one can rise through study to be a Master Mason. Their organizational structure, based upon the old axiom of the Raman Artificers, who claimed that it required three to make a college (*tres faciuni collegiums*), in all degree levels involve three principal officers, three supports, three greater and three lesser lights.... Referring to the prominence of the number 3 in Druidism, and in the ancient pre-Christian rites of Mithra, which were supported by three intelligences—Mithra, Ormuad, and Mithras—Masons adopted the belief it was "a general character of the mysteries to have three principal officers and three grades of initiation." Masons also utilize in their rituals:

The Power of the Three

- Threefold Chord.
- Three Fires.
- Three Globes.
- Three Grand Offerings.
- Three Points of a Triangle.
- Three Sacred Utensils.
- Three Senses (seeing, hearing, and feeling).

3 in Folklore and Fairytales

Mystical and esoteric traditions often adopt the wisdom teachings of many ancient cultures, recognizing commonalities in symbols, archetypes, and images. Religions, major and minor, new and old, are often built upon the pagan beliefs that existed far before them. No matter where we turn we are greeted with the number 3 in some form or another, to the point that it has actually become a part of our language, and the way we understand wisdom and learn the lessons of our human-ness. We often do that through story, and nowhere is this more present—this power of the three—than in fairytales and folklore.

Why on earth were there three little pigs, and not four? Why were there three billy goats gruff crossing the troll bridge, and not two? Was there a reason that there were only three blind mice and not a whole slew of them?

It begins: Once upon a time, there were three little pigs. The first pig built a house of straw, the second a house of sticks, the third a house of bricks. Along comes the big bad wolf, who is hungry for some tasty pork. He blows down the first house and eats the first pig. He is still hungry, and blows down the second house, feasting upon the second pig. Still not satiated, the wolf goes to the third house, the house of bricks.

"Little pig, little pig, let me come in!"

"Not by the hair of your chinny-chin-chin!"

"Then I'll huff, and I'll puff and I'll blow your house in."

The Trinity Secret

Only the brick house won't be moved, no matter how hard the wolf blows and huffs and puffs. He tries to trick the third pig out of his fortress, but the third pig eludes him each time. Eventually, the wolf decides to go down the chimney, determined to have pork for dessert, and instead, he ends up dropping into a pot of boiling water and becomes wolf stew for a very hungry pig.

This fairytale, which allegedly dates back to the 1840s in a book called *Nursery Rhymes and Nursery Tales* by James Orchard Halliwell-Phillips, has other variations in which the first two pigs end up running out of their homes and to the third pig's home for safety, although critics suggest this was a blatant later attempt to avoid the violence of the original version. Why such a violent and horrific story, and one labeled a "nursery rhyme" at that? Well, we can start with the common theme of a young one leaving home for the first time, and entering the big, bad world of danger, in order to become an adult.

An example of this comes from the pre-Christian Mithraism, a Roman mystery religion that was popular in every corner of the Roman Empire between the late second century BC to approximately AD 400. This was the last pagan religion in Europe before Christianity took over, and many scholars equate the story of Mithras with many of the legends surrounding Christ. The spiritual and philosophical tenets of Mithraism closely parallel early Christian teachings, including the virgin birth of Mithras in a cave on December 25, the same date later attached to the birth of Christ.

In one of the Mithraic fairlytales, called "Simorgh," the hero, the young Prince Khorshid (Mithra), has no mother, but is the bravest of his three brothers, and beloved by the king. The story follows the prince as he encounters many challenges, and closely mirrors other Indo-European tripartite ideology found in many stories of heroes, Gods, Goddesses, demons, princes, and princesses—always in threes. They may be the three Brahman classes of priest, warrior, and producer; the three segments of Celtic society of Druid priests, Flaith warriors, and Boarig herders; or, as in the "Simorgh," with a hero who will fight three demons or a beast with three heads or take on three challenges. Some scholars suggest this ideology has survived today in the use of three

The Power of the Three

colors in the flags of many Indo-European nations, including France, Germany, Bulgaria, Russia, Syria, Armenia, the UK, the United States, Lithuania, Afghanistan, and others.

But the use of the number 3 signifies something beyond just another "Hero's Journey," this time with pigs instead of science fiction heroes (a la Luke Skywalker). How about the story of the Three Billy Goats Gruff? This Norwegian fairytale was included in a collection of stories called *Norske Fokeeventyr*, translated to English; Peter Christen Asbjornsen and Jorgen Moe wrote the original version. The story starts out with three goats: a young, small goat; a medium-sized adult goat; and an older, bigger, and wiser goat. Often these goats are described as brothers, other times as child, father, and grandfather. The gist of the story is this: the first goat attempts to cross a bridge to find new grass to eat and get nice and fat. The first goat crosses the bridge, but is stopped by the sound of a mean troll, who says "Click, clack, click, clack, who is that crossing my bridge?"

The first goat introduces himself, but the troll threatens in return to "gobble him up." Cleverly, the first goat convinces the troll to hold off, for his bigger, meatier "brother" goat is coming. The troll, being greedy, agrees and lets the first goat cross. Along comes the second goat. He's bigger, but the troll still throws out the same threat. The second goat talks the troll into waiting for the third goat, because he will be the meatiest yet. The troll lets him on by. Now comes the third goat—big, meaty, and tough. Up to the bridge he goes, and the troll once again threatens to gobble him up. The third goat will have none of it and tosses the little, ugly troll into the water. The goats find a lush field of grass to feed upon, and the troll is taken downriver.

If you recall from your childhood, Jack climbs the beanstalk three times, the wicked stepmother pays a visit to the lovely Snow White three times before she causes her death, and Rumpelstiltskin spins three times for the beautiful princess and lets her guess his name three times, and Cinderella goes to the ball three times before striking gold with the prince.

And who can forget the three bears and Goldilocks? It's the story of a small baby bear, a middle-sized mama bear, and a big daddy bear who go for a walk one day, only to come back to find some chick named Goldilocks has committed a home invasion and tried all of their chairs, beds, and oatmeal before being chased outside by three pissed-off bears. In the story,

Fig. 5-2   Goldilocks is never satisfied with the first two things she tries, and always settles on the third, whether it be the chair, the bed, or the oatmeal.

These stories don't just resonate as lessons to be learned, but also as a means of pattern recognition whereby they become ingrained in our brains and our psyches. For maximum impact, whether in story, speech, or language, you absolutely must do it three times. Folk and fairytales often include a task or action the hero or heroine must do three times in order to achieve a particular goal. Not once, not twice, three times a lady—oh wait, sorry...

The Rule of Three

It is called the Rule of Three. Maximum humor, impact, drama, or effect seems to happen when we hear, say, or do something three times. This principle of writing and speech suggests that when you repeat

The Power of the Three

something, or group things together by threes in a sentence, or say three phrases, it has far more emotional and cerebral impact. Think "Go, fight, win!" Or, as realtors love to say, "Location, location, location." Perhaps the most famous of these is "Veni, vidi, vici" ("I came, I saw, I conquered"), as spoken by Julius Caesar. Variations of this include the "tricolon," or sentence with three defined parts (cola) of equal length and increasing power. Again, the words of Caesar speak of a progression from weak to strong—"I came" to "I conquered." Lincoln used tricolons in his Gettysburg Address with "of the people, by the people, for the people," and in his second inaugural address, and no doubt every president after him has noted the power of using tricolons in speeches. Even the use of three-word phrases has been recognized as being the most important key to obtaining maximum impact. Think of George Bush, Sr., with "Read my lips. No new taxes!" He liked it so much he did it twice!

Another variation is called Hendiatris, from the Greek for "one through three." This figure of speech also utilized three words or phrases to express a singular idea. Think "wine, women, and song" or "Chevy, Coke, and apple pie," or even "God, country, and King." Hitler employed a tripartite slogan with "Ein Volk! Ein Reich! Ein Fuhrer!" which meant "One people! One state! One leader!" In Hitler's case the progression is bitterly ironic, as the importance of himself was the endpoint, rather than the greater importance of the people in general.

The Rule of Three builds tension in a progression that leads up to a very satisfying end point. Whether that endpoint is the punch line of a joke, or the final scene in a fairytale, it's the third beat that packs the power. Two elements are not enough, for it takes a minimum of three to establish a recognizable pattern. And boy, do our brains love patterns. The average movie, if written well, has a three-act structure, as do plays and even, in a sense, novels: beginning, middle, and end, with the end as the most satisfying element, completing the progression. It can even imply "contrasting threes," as in the fairytales where three elements are presented and one wins out (the third pig's house, the third billy goat). The winning element is such a contrast from the first element presented, but again it is presented in a pattern that we recognize and are drawn to.

The Trinity Secret

Again, the third time is the charm. Would the following quote have the same impact with only two things, or how about four or five?

> When you die, only three things will remain of you, since you will abandon all material things on the threshold of the Otherworld: what you have taught to others, what you have created with your hands, and how much love you have spread.
> —Francois Bourillon

The rhythm created by threes, and the symbolic aspects that we instinctually react to, convey a message much more powerfully and sufficiently than any other quantity could.

Have one little pig, and you have no story. Have four little pigs, and boredom or tediousness ensues. But, like the porridge Goldilocks taste-tests, the third one is "just right."

Before the development of modern-day number systems, we might theorize that prehistoric people counted by less specific means. One was one, two was two, and all beyond that was "many." Until the need arose for more detailed ways of measuring quantity, "many" was as sufficient as our current use of the word *few* is to indicate more than two. In the art of storytelling, most notably in fairytales, the use of three characters, tasks, incidents, or objects plays into the human brain's need to seek out a pattern that has meaning. According to Max Luthi, author of *The Fairy Tale as Art Form and Portrait of Man*, that meaning may come from another need: the need for security. He writes, "The number gives security not only to the narrator, who relies on it and takes pleasure in making use of it, but to the listener, as well." Three implies the most basic family unit, the wholeness of encompassing opposites, the perfection and completeness of life itself. Heroes and heroines, even those in animal form, were always being tested or challenged in some way to attempt to achieve order out of chaos. We learn from these structured stories how to be human, how to stand up to fear, dissipate evil, and grab the brass ring. According to K. Sean Buvals in "The Presence of the Number Three in Folktales" on Storyteller.net, "In storytelling, chaos results when player one and player two attempt to succeed at a task, but

The Power of the Three

through their own failure or moral shortcomings are unable to complete that task. Then the third player, naturally more powerful than the first two, succeeds at the task, succeeds at the perfection of the story." Pig number three had the only house that stood up to the wolf, and a plan to cook the canid as well!

Three also serves to provide balance between two extremes, perhaps youngest to older to oldest. Jung is cited as saying that every tension of opposites culminates in a release, and out of this release comes the third, ending the tension and resolving unity. Without an ending, the beginning and middle are moot points. Perhaps this is why movies and novels that end on ambiguous notes are not as satisfying at those that end with a perfectly discernable conclusion, whether happily ever after or "oh man, she died."

According to a Russian proverb, "God loves the Three."

Three doesn't stop at fairytales, though. Shakespeare utilized the power of three, as did many other playwrights and great storytellers of old. Some scholars suggest this is because the spoken word, during a play, was repeated three times, once to each side of the audience and again to those in the center aisles. And of course, there are the jokes—you know, "Three men walk into a bar…." "A priest, a rabbi, and a monk…." As Buvals points out, the moral of the persistence of three may be to show the two sides, two options, and then show the truth that exists in between. Meaning that one of those guys who walks into the bar will most likely be wiser, clearer, and more likely to "complete" the joke. Oh, and you could always replace the priest, rabbi, and monk with a blonde, a brunette, and a redhead.

Cultural Implications of the Number 3

But how much of this is natural, and how much of this is cultural? In a fascinating article titled "The Number Three in American Culture," the late Professor Alan Dundes of Berkeley University dissects the fascination with all things that come in three. Students of anthropology are called upon to understand the nature of other cultures, but more importantly the nature of their own culture. Dundes points out the pattern of use of three in Greek and Roman culture, as well as classical literature, law, and even medicine, pointing to the existence of this pattern in most of the Western world, as well as Indo-European culture.

Much of this evidence is found in religion and mythology, with the prevalence of triads of Gods, deities with three heads, and triune divinities that expressed the three-into-one Trinitarian Concept. Dundes refers to this "three-determinism" as just as visible today as it was in more ancient times, pointing to the work of Raimund Muller in examining modern European's 3-focused culture. American culture has adopted the importance of 3 in ritual, although Dundes is quick to point out that other numbers—notably 4,5, and 7—also play large roles in European, Native American, and modern American cultures. Also, he cites dualism in the form of famous twos worldwide, as in the anatomy of the human body, with two arms, legs, ears, eyes, and so forth: "The present thesis is not that the number three is the only numerical native category in American culture, but rather that it is the predominant one."

Many Native American tribes revere the number 4, representing the four cardinal signs, the four wind directions, and seeing the world not through a triune lens, but a fourfold one. Perhaps the power of three that permeates American culture is a direct result of the pre-Christian and Christian evolution of thought about the Trinity, which would not have infiltrated native culture. Some of Dundes's examples of the nature of "trichotomy" in modern culture include things we all understand:

1. Three is an absolute limit, in terms and categorizations.
2. The alphabet itself is referred to as the ABCs—only three letters to summarize the whole.
3. Shirts normally come in small, medium, and large. (Extra-large is a derivative of large.)
4. Golf has under par, par, and over par.
5. Airport arrivals are broken into early, on time, and late!
6. Sports are filled with threes and groups of threes, with nine innings, nine players, three outs, three strikes (oops—four balls???).

The Power of the Three

7. In football, a field goal is three points, and a touchdown is six.
8. Boxing rounds are three minutes in duration.

These examples imply the way threes and groupings by threes have become a part of our language, behavior, and common understanding. We win, lose, or draw, and only the first three racers get the recognition: win, place, and show. Gold, silver, and bronze. Even our insistence at naming organizations shows up in threes: CBS, NBC, AAA, KKK, AMA, PTA, CIA, FBI. And of course, we do all we can to not be DOA, or TKO, although at some point we hope to RIP. If we need help, we can always SOS, unless there is no civilization in sight. Then we are SOL. You could while away the time playing tic-tac-toe, or, if trapped, blow up the wall with TNT, but be sure there is someone from FOX to cover it on the nightly news while viewers are home eating breakfast, lunch, or dinner!

Again, though, nowhere is this prevalence more, well, prevalent than in our folklore. We took a look at fairytales, and all the reasons why repetition in threes impacts us on a gut and heart level. How about all those folk songs, though? Does the same Rule of Three apply?

"Mary had a little lamb, little lamb, little lamb…."

"London Bridge is falling down, falling down, falling down…."

"One little, two little, three little Indians…."

"Go tell it on the mountain, go tell it on the mountain, go tell it on the mountain…."

This use of 3 is called trebling in folk songs and again serves to use repetition to give the song more impact, not to mention a satisfying rhythm. Superstitions and riddles also adopt this same concept:

"Three times a bridesmaid, never a bride."

"Third time's a charm."

Even our view on the human life span comes in three, as in the Riddle of the Sphinx, "What walks first on four legs, then on two legs, then on three?" Us! When we sing, tell stories, or impart beliefs, we want the receiver to get the point and understand what we are trying to say. It is this simple. Singing it, doing it, and saying it three times does the trick, or, as in the case of marriage, avoiding it.

The Trinity Secret

We shall overcome! Up, up, and away! I like Ike! Seize the day!

Our entire education system is based upon primary, secondary, and higher education. We go to school to learn the three Rs: readin', 'riting, and 'rithmetic. Hopefully one day we will get our bachelor's, master's, and doctoral degrees—depending, of course, on how well our teachers followed the "preview, teach, review" method of imparting knowledge.

We could go on like this for pages and pages. In a cultural sense, we live according to numbers, and the one we live according to the most is 3. It may be hard-wired into our brain as a pattern we recognize from the times of our ancestors, or an intuitive recognition of the triune nature of creation and reality, which we will explore more soon. Dundes points out that we as humans relate to nature in three ways: as less than, or subjugated to, nature; as equal to nature; and as superior, or super-ordinate, to nature. Maybe our attempts to communicate come from the sense that we are of three minds: inferior, equal, and superior to others around us, and we often need a way to relate in three ways. Even the scholars ask: Is this obsession with 3 the result of our focus on the family unit of father, mother, and child as the wholeness of life? Or the archetypal understanding of our universe based upon our need to see and identify dualities (cold, hot; dark, light; day, night) and then unify them into a single entity or whole?

Maybe, just maybe, we recognize that in the power of 3 is a deeper power—one that speaks of not only how we got here, but how we create everything else around us. Maybe, just maybe, we know that 3 stands for something so profound, and yet so simple, that it can't help but find its way into our culture, our stories, our myths, our songs, and even our baseball games. Even in our archeological ages, with stone, bronze, and iron. Not to mention how we judge a woman's body with waist, hip, and bust measurements. It is just *that* pervasive.

Listen to our language, the spoken and the unspoken, and see.

"It is written."

"Snip, snap, snout.
   This chapter's told out!"

The Power of the Three

6 As Above, So Below: The Science of the Trinity

Simplicity is the ultimate sophistication.
—Leonardo da Vinci

The reason why the universe is eternal is that it does not live for itself; it gives life to others as it transforms.
—Lao Tzu

Some 40 years after physicist Vitaly Efimov predicted that particles could and should be able to form an arrangement known as the Borromean rings, physicists at Rice University in Houston managed to do exactly that. Led by Randy Hulet, the team of physicists set up a "Feshbach resonance," which allowed them to tweak energy levels of a set of three bound lithium atoms. When they used a binding energy of 515, which indicates how tightly the particles hold onto one another and how much energy is needed to pull them apart, the particles would bind, but would not do so at other energies. The scientists proved that three particles, whether atoms, protons, or even quarks, could be bound together in a stable state, but two of them could not. It required the third particle to create the triplet, and Efimov had even predicted that the bound states could achieve even higher and higher energy levels, again all based upon multiples of 515.

Although this may not sound very important in the grand scheme of things, it definitely takes on a more profound effect when we learn that the symbol for this ancient mathematical principle has its own unique link to the Trinity of Christianity. The Borromean rings are symmetrical arrangements of three intersecting circles where no two rings are completely linked, so if any one of the rings is cut, all three rings fall apart. The union, or whole, then becomes more important than any of the individual rings, yet the rings are still a part of the whole, playing their role in keeping the ring together. This symbol, named after the Borromeo family in Italy, who used the symbol on their coat of arms, was found in Gandharva Buddhist art dating back to the second century AD.

The same imagery is found in Norse image stones and the art of Michelangelo, and even serves as the symbol for Ballentine Beer.

Perhaps one of the strangest aspects of the rings is the association with the I Ching. The rings can be interlaced by replacing each of the six vertices by a crossing indicating how the circles pass over and under each other. There are two choices for each crossing, therefore there are a total of 2^6 or 64 possible interlaced patterns. The I Ching consists of a set of oracular statements represented by 64 sets of six lines each called *hexagrams*. Each hexagram is a figure composed of six stacked horizontal lines; each line is either *yang* (an *unbroken* or *solid* line), or *yin* (*broken, open* line with a gap in the center). With six such lines stacked from bottom to top there are 26 or 64 possible combinations, and thus 64 hexagrams represented, just as in the Borromean rings.

Four variations of the Borromean rings.

Fig. 6-1, 6-2, 6-3, 6-4

The same concept has also been associated with the Trinity itself, based on an illustration in a 13th-century French manuscript found at Chartres, as reproduced in art historian/archeologist Adolphe Didron's book, *Christian Iconography* (1843). In this version, the rings are fully sealed off and interlocking. The idea of three interlaced entities that, if one were to be removed, extinguished all three, is paralleled to the idea that if one aspect of the Trinity were removed, there would be no whole, no all, no unification of the three. Father, Son, Holy Spirit. Remove one and the others crumble. If the Trinity itself represents an archetype of creation, then we can see how removing one aspect would not allow for creation to exist.

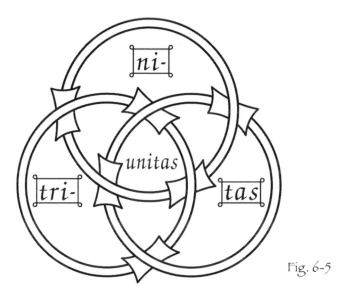

Fig. 6-5

TRINITAS is around the edge, and UNITAS in the center.

Lacan's Triune Reality

This Trinity of circles also apparently inspired Jacques Lacan (April 13, 1901–September 9, 1981) as a model of the topology of human subjectivity. Lacan was a French psychoanalyst and psychiatrist who created this model in 1953 using each ring to represent a component

As Above, So Below

of his idea of the orders of reality—the real, the imaginary, and the symbolic. He was influenced by the teachings of Freud, but had a fascination with the rings and with knot theory. Like Freud's id, ego, and superego, Lacan's threefold reality was an attempt to reinterpret the whole of psychoanalytic theory in terms of the Borromean rings and related concepts behind the mathematics of knot theory, a branch of topology that deals with knots and links (yes, this really does exist!).

If we look at the orders of Lacan's reality, we find a strong resemblance to the orders of reality described by physicist David Bohm. Bohm became deeply interested in quantum physics in the 1930s while attending Pennsylvania State College (now University). After receiving his doctorate at the University of California, Berkeley, he began working on plasmas (gas containing high densities of electrons and positive ions). His work with plasma opened his eyes to a larger and interconnected order based upon the behavior of electrons in a plasma, which stop behaving in an individual fashion and start behaving more like a part of a greater whole.

Bohm continued his research projects at Princeton, and in 1951 he wrote the book *Quantum Theory*, which became the standard textbook describing the Copenhagen Interpretation of quantum physics. Nevertheless, Bohm had suspicions that, underneath this widely accepted interpretation, there were unanswered questions about the behavior of particles. He was not convinced that particles only did what they did by chance, and that the quantum world was one of randomness and absolute indeterminism. In fact, Bohm intuited a deeper cause and a deeper order. He sent his book to colleagues Niels Bohr and Albert Einstein. Surprisingly Bohm only got a response from Einstein, who was open to discussion.

For a period of about six months, Bohm and Einstein discussed their dissatisfaction with orthodox quantum theory as well as their general discomfort with the idea that what they knew was all there was to know of the quantum world. Bohm continued his studies, even enduring troubles with McCarthyism, which he refused to partake in, eventually resulting in his having to seek work outside of the United States. In 1952, he published two papers that would ultimately serve as the foundation of his "causal interpretation of quantum theory," rejecting the current belief that subatomic particles were simple, structure-less, and without purpose or direction. Bohm's work recognized a subtle force underlying quantum behavior, which he called the "quantum potential," and suggested this force actually directed particles by giving them information about their environment.

This quantum potential was everywhere, permeating all of space, and allowed for a connectedness to all quantum systems. Further experiments with Yakir Aharonov in 1959 showed that electrons can sometimes sense the presence of a magnetic field even if they are in a region of space where the field strength is zero. To this day, his fairly controversial study, named the Aharonov-Bohm Effect, does not have a clear consensus, with many in the scientific community disagreeing with its findings. But Bohm pressed on, and another physicist took up his cause in 1982, which led to a groundbreaking research experiment that would test, and ultimately prove, that this quantum connectedness existed.

Led by physicist Alain Aspect, a team of physicists put to the test the ideas of Eistein, Bohm, and other scientific notables such as John Bell of CERN in Geneva, all of whom contributed to the theoretical foundation of this connectedness principle. The end results proved clearly that subatomic particles, even when separated by vast geographic distances, could communicate in a manner that is not explained by physical signals traveling at or below the speed of light. In fact, these "non-local" communications appeared to be instantaneous! This research, in addition to Bohm's further exploration into order, and what he called the "holomovement," endeavored to answer the questions once posed regarding the contradictions between quantum mechanics and relativity theory. The holomovement concept suggested that the Universe was like a giant, flowing hologram, and that total order could be found on a deeper level in any part of the space/time continuum. Just in the way that a holograph can be dismantled yet retain the total image in each dismantled piece, the implicit order of the Universe did as well, and what we deem as our physical world is in fact projected from some higher level or order of reality. Plato once said, "The Universe is a single whole, composed of many parts that are also wholes." This holographic concept is not new!

As Above, So Below

Unfoldment in the Holomovement

To Bohm, the nature of physical reality was wholeness, oneness, rather than a collection of individual objects. This whole was, on some order, undivided, although we see ourselves as well as the world around us through the eyes of "separateness." The holomovement suggests that reality is in a constant state of change and flux, but again structured like a hologram, with each part of physical reality containing the entirety of information of the whole. There was a process of enfoldment and unfoldment by which the universe generated itself, and life and consciousness were an integral part of that enfoldment. This enfoldment and unfoldment occurred on the first order—the implicate—and are made manifest in the second order—the explicate, the domain of matter. Both make up the fundamental aspects of the holomovement. Bohm states in *Wholeness and the Implicate Order* that a particle is "an abstraction that is manifest to our senses. What is, is always a totality of ensembles, all present together, in an orderly series of stages of enfoldment and unfoldment, which intermingle and interpenetrate each other in principle throughout the whole of space."

Bohm's cosmology consisted of three orders, starting with the implicate order. The first, the invisible, unseen realm or "hidden order" is that which we do not see at work when we look at something as happening by chance, coincidence, synchronistically. The explicate order is the apparent manifestation of matter in physical form, the surface appearance of what occurs on the invisible level of the implicate. In Bohm's view, space, time, and matter are all connected, and the idea of empty space does not exist. Bohm states that space has so much energy and is "rather full than empty," something that recent experiments with Zero Point Energy fully support. A single cubic centimeter of empty space containing Zero Point Energy contains more energy that all the matter of the known universe! There is no empty.

Bohm used the analogy of a flowing stream to describe the relationship between the separate objects, beings, entities, and structures that are visible on the physical level of the explicate and the deeper order of unbroken wholeness from where they came.

On this stream, one may see an ever-changing pattern of vortices, ripples, waves, splashes, etc., which evidently have no independent existence as such. Rather, they are abstracted from the flowing movement, arising and vanishing in the total process of the flow. Such transitory subsistence as may be possessed by these abstracted forms implies only a relative independence or autonomy of behavior, rather than absolutely independent existence as ultimate substances.

In Bohm's cosmology, the enfolded, or implicate order was a place where space and time no longer served as the dominant factors for determining relationships of dependence and interdependence of different elements. There was instead a more basic connection of these elements, from which our notions of space and time and material form and matter are "abstracted as forms from the deeper order." These notions are the explicate order, yet contained within the totality of the implicate.

If we think of Carl Jung's work with synchronicity, we see the same concept of the cause of synchronistic experiences or events as occurring on the hidden, implicate level, where we cannot see them. What we see are the events unfolding in the explicate, and wonder at how such events could possibly be connected. But they are—in the implicate. These concepts he referred to as the "acausal connecting principle," a principle at work on a deeper level that to us appears miraculous, without cause. Synchronicities represent something that unfolds in the deeper orders, and manifest in our world as linked, meaningful "coincidences."

The Implicate Order

Of the three levels or order, or reality (the third of which we will get to very soon!), the implicate is the most fascinating. We have familiarity with the explicate, we live in the explicate, yet when we stop to ask ourselves where it, and we, came from and how it all got here, we are forced to enter the world of the implicate. Like Bohm, we seek to focus on the order of wholeness instead of the order of the separate parts.

As Above, So Below

Bohm's implicate order could be equated with the Kingdom of Heaven spoken of. This is the order that we ourselves are immersed in, yet we do not see it. Instead, our focus is on the material, physical manifestations. Hermes spoke of the implicate in the lost wisdom of the Hermetica, the studies and teachings he imparted, when he said:

In a sense, the Cosmos is changeless,
because its motions are determined by unalterable laws
which cause it to revolve eternally
without beginning and end.
Its parts manifest, disappear and are created anew,
Again and again
In the undulating pulse of time.

Thus, the ongoing enfoldment, and unfoldment, that continuously creates manifest life, matter, form, and structure revolving eternally without beginning or end.

There are other names this order may go by. We have written extensively about the Zero Point Field, and our own take on an infrastructure of reality that we call the Grid. In either case, we are talking about a field of all potentiality, a field of all possibility. A field that is the wholeness in which all else comes from, exists in, and returns to.

This field, written about extensively by author Lynne McTaggart in *The Field: The Quest for the Secret Force of the Universe* and *The Intention Experiment*, connects everything in the universe to everything else as a dynamic energy network that we ourselves are a part of. Embracing everything from psychic phenomena, healing, alternative medicine, the paranormal, and how thought shapes reality, McTaggart's exploration of the field also paralleled the teachings of many primitive cultures that long ago recognized the interconnectedness of all life—that we were all strands in the web of reality. Consciousness plays a huge role, with the notion that the unconscious mind, or the subconscious, held the power to communicate with the unseen world, or in this case the "subtangible physical world—the quantum world of all possibility," linking the observer to the effects of reality just as is seen in the quantum experiment. The field, therefore, is the mental and physical world, with no distinction between the two, at least on the implicate order of the field. The way it might work is described in the book as "the marriage of unformed mind and matter would then assemble itself into something tangible in the manifest world." The enfolding, and unfolding, from the implicate to the explicate. Something out of nothing.

From *The Field*, one of the pioneers of research into the Zero Point Field and Zero Point Energy is nuclear physicist Hal Puthoff, who described the field as "a kind of self-regenerating grand ground state of the universe" constantly refreshing itself, linking us and all other matter in the Universe in an invisible bond of "waves of the grandest dimensions."

Physicist F. David Peat, in his book *Synchronicity: The Bridge Between Mind and Matter*, refers to this hidden field as a complex "active field of information that unfolds in the various structures and processes of nature, and of matter that has endless levels of subtlety," and, as suggested by Jung's archetypes, "may act in both consciousness and matter so that the deeper the mind is explored, the more complex is its structure." Peat proposes that this hidden order is closer to a form of intelligence than just a field of habitual responses and may have an "underlying creative source."

The enfolding and unfolding of Bohm's implicate order acts in both directions: of mental to the material aspects of nature, and material to the mental. Peat continues that information from this hidden field is impressed upon the material process so that they are "structured or informed by it." This also works in the reverse, with explicate structures resulting in the "information content of the deeper order." Thus, the material (explicate) level is perceived by the mental level (implicate), which then acts back on the unfolding of the material side. This is the constant and active process of creation.

"Reality," Peat suggests, is pictured as a "limitless series of levels that extend to deeper and deeper subtleties and out of which the particular, explicate order of nature and the order of consciousness and life emerge."

As Above, So Below

Carl Jung and the Pleroma

This implicate reality is also mirrored in Carl Jung's *Pleroma*, an ancient term used to describe a ground state or "Godhead" from which reality comes, a nothingness that is "both empty and full," an infinite and eternal state that embodies no qualities, because it embodies all qualities. All dualities exist, yet they cease to exist in the Pleroma. From this formless, endless Pleroma, the world of Creatura, order, and distinction, arises. Pleroma does not change, but Creatura is constantly changing and contains the reality of mind and matter in the Universe.

Ralph Abraham, mathematician and pioneer of chaos theory, writes in *The Evolutionary Mind* of his space/time model of reality: "the space/time continuum with all phenomena attached, including individual consciousness, the morphogenetic field, the wave functions of quantum mechanics, and the extra dimensions of the image, and so on." He suggests we call it the Logos, the word, the sound of creation. The morphogenetic field he refers to is the work of Rupert Sheldrake, a biologist and author of *The Sense of Being Stared At, and Other Aspects of the Extended Mind.* This field is actually a subset of the morphic field that Sheldrake proposes, a field within and around a "morphic unit" that organizes its characteristic structure and pattern of activity. A particular form that is a member of a group that has established that particular morphic field can tune into this field of collective information. In other words, a form can tap into the collective "dumping ground" of information already established by its group and provide feedback to the field, adding to the database of information and experience. This allows the morphic field to grow in both organic and abstract forms.

The idea of a universal database is also found in Vedic literature as the Akashic Records, or library of all human experiences and memories. Carl Jung referred to it as the collective unconscious, from which archetype was born, and accessed. Author and Nobel Peace Prize nominee Ervin Laszlo writes about the Akashic Field in *The Akashic Experience: Science and the Cosmic Memory Field*. Lazlo, a systems theorist, gathered 20 leading authorities in their fields to discuss firsthand accounts of this "cosmic memory field" that is able to transmit information to people without use of the senses.

Akasha is an ancient Hindu concept that describes the fundamental nature of the cosmos as ether containing the material and nonmaterial. The idea that any experience in nature could not be "lost" led to the concept of Akashic Records, the recording of life experiences upon a field, where these experiences and memories could be accessed using means outside of the five senses, such as intuition or meditation. As the quantum holographic information continuously feeds into the field, more information is exponentially created—generating, creating, coming into manifest order.

Entanglement in the Akasha

Quantum entanglement or non-locality also bonds us in a web of connectedness in the field. We, like particles, become entangled and remain able to communicate with each other across space and time, instantaneously, each affecting the other. There is a body of scientific research showing that particles that at any time occupied the same quantum state can remain correlated with each other, no matter the amount of time or space in between. They stay entangled, even when no longer considered "local" to one another.

There is no separation in the Akasha. This is the realm of what Laszlo calls the "non-local mind"—the mind that is "infinite and space and time, unconfined and unconfinable to the here-and-now." From this field where non-local mind exists, we can extract information from the past, present, or future, because here there is no such thing as linear time. We can see into the past, predict the future, remote view, communicate with the deceased, visit other realities, and even heal at a distance. Using the part of the human mind that is not limited by time and space as we know it in the explicate order, we tap into the

As Above, So Below

records of collective information, always being added to, enfolding, and unfolding to create more information. Beyond our sensory contact lies the realm of psychic ability, where we quite simply acquire information from the vast resources of the field, the vast storehouse of records. British author David Lorimer calls this "empathic resonance," harking back to Sheldrake's morphic resonance.

In his book *Whole in One: The Near-Death Experience and the Ethic of Interconnectedness*, Lorimer examines the phenomenon of NDE and finds correlations between the reported empathic life review to various psychic phenomena and to the mystic's "oneness" and connectedness of all life. Lorimer sees this as a universal "empathic resonance," that implies a set of ethics that recognizes the wholeness of all things. Sort of a "collective ethic" we all aspire to follow, as in the Golden Rule of "Do Unto Others."

Laszlo suggests that the ability for non-local mental functioning may actually be encoded within our DNA as part of our evolutionary ascent. This ability would no doubt serve us well to help ward off or predict dangerous situations, as well as help us intuit where to find food, shelter and water. If this is inherent ability in all of us, then that means we all have the ability to walk the field, travel the Grid, and search the hall of records for information we seek that cannot be found anywhere in the manifest world.

Laszlo summarizes the Akashic Field as a field of quantum holograms, like a superconducting "cosmic medium": "There is nothing in that field that could impede the frictionless spread and entanglement of the holograms that arise in it. The quantum holograms created by the waves emitted by objects in space and time entangle through the field—that is, throughout space and time." These waves go on to produce sequences of interference patterns that end in the superhologram, the integration of all other holograms. The superhologram carries information on all the things that exist and have ever existed, and, as Laszlo states, becomes the "hologram of the universe."

The implicate order and its other identities, the field, Grid, what have you, is the most critical order behind the manifestation of physical creation. Critical because it is in this order that there is an action, a process by which nothing is turned into something. No thing into some thing. In the implicate order exists the activating agent by which creation is created. Without this "middle order" there is no creation, only potentiality, superposition, probability, possibility.

The Links to the Trinity

What does all of this have to do with the Trinity, you may be asking? The implicate order, the field, the Grid, or the Akasha is one of the three parts of the Trinity itself. It is probably obvious by now that if we look at Bohm's orders, we can identify the explicate as the physical, the creation, and the implicate as the creative force itself. Thus, the explicate becomes the Son, the Christ as creation made manifest in the physical world. In a sense, this is the least intriguing of the three parts of the whole, for we all recognize the physical, and acknowledge the manifest. The Son of the Trinity, the Creation, the end result, is not so much a mystery as the first two parts of the whole.

The implicate, the hidden world of cause and generation and enfolding and unfolding, the field of information and hall of records of experience is the Holy Spirit. We will examine the Holy Spirit more in depth in a later chapter, but let's get back to Bohm for a moment. Because the Trinity is not complete until we ask: What about the Father? What about the third and perhaps most important element? Did Bohm have an order for God?

He sure did!

In 1987, Bohm wrote a book called *Science, Order and Creativity* with physicist F. David Peat. The book was based upon discussions between Bohm and Peat, and resulted in Bohm's concept of a super-implicate order. If the implicate order, or as he called it here, the first implicate order, is the original field, then the superimplicate or second implicate order is "a superfield of information that guides and organizes the original field." It is an extension of the implicate order, that which surrounds, interpenetrates, and underlies the implicate order. A super order, above and beyond the other two, but encompassing both as well. Like the Godhead of the Trinity, the Father held the supreme position,

As Above, So Below

yet the Son and Holy Spirit are a part of the Father and encompassed with the Father.

In terms of quantum theory, where the implicate order acts as the field, the superimplicate would therefore be the superquantum potential, with the explicate order simply the measurable and observable effects of what goes on in the other two orders. In this higher order, a particle is just an abstraction in the human mind, part of the holomovement between the ever-changing implicate order (quantum field) and the superquantum potential (superimplicate order). The particle itself then becomes the explicate effect. Think back to Laszlo's superhologram that contains all the information of everything that has existed, and ever will. In the superimplicate we find a sort of coded record of everything that has taken place in space and time, from the Big Bang and before, to the end of time, and possibly beyond.

Are there other, even higher implicate orders? Maybe so, but to Bohm, if that were the case, the effects of these higher orders might be increasingly subtle and difficult to ever observe. Maybe these higher orders actually do exist, and provide the implicate order with the potential to manifest novelty in the explicate.

To Bohm, reality was shaped and molded in the implicate and superimplicate orders. The explicate was simply the end result. The manifestation of the activities of the unseen orders. Bohm likened the manifest world to the ripples in a pond when an invisible stone is tossed in. We don't see the stone, but we see the ripples, and can therefore conclude that the stone existed—that the stone was causality. Perhaps one of Bohm's most famous statements is "The electron, in-so-far as it responds to a meaning in its environment, is observing the environment. It is doing exactly what human beings are doing." As Above, So Below.

The superimplicate order is like heaven, beyond ordinary perception, eternal and existing beyond the grip of time; in fact, it is outside of time. It is a creative order, and that creativity flows down to the other lower orders, eventually becoming manifest in the time-based world of the explicate. Bohm described this highest order as "eternally fresh and new," but eventually directed toward the "temporal or secular order."

Though we cannot actually see this undivided wholeness, we can see its effects in our everyday lives. Bohm stated that theories in science are "forms of insights that arise in our attempts to obtain a perception of a deeper nature of reality as a whole." That form of perception may be locked inside our brains, or perhaps just outside of the brain, as human consciousness. This will be explored more fully in the next chapter.

And if this wholeness contains all the information of the past, present, and future, as suggested by the Akasha, the field, and the Grid, we, then, could have already found ways to tap into this invisible order and access what we seek in order to heal, to see beyond the range of the human eye, to discern higher wisdom, to locate hidden objects, to communicate with those far away, and to see into our individual and collective past and future. Those in the paranormal and metaphysical fields believe that they have been doing this all along. Those who have studied the ancient knowledge and wisdom of the yogis, the Mayans, the Greeks, and the Sumerians, know that we, as a species, have been aware of these three orders of reality all along. However, we may not have understood—truly understood—our connection to these orders, and how we ourselves might be using them as well: to create our reality just as the higher force we may refer to as God, Master Architect, Source, or just the All, uses them to create our Universe.

Blackfoot Physics, and Bohm's Orders

Science and spirit seem to come together in this concept, and Bohm knew that well. He spent significant amounts of time with mystics and sages, talking ideas, comparing notes. Remarkably, even other physicists have looked to non-scientific cultures to glean common ground. Theoretical physicist F. David Peat spent time with the Blackfoot Indians, learning about their cosmology and worldview, and finding stunning correlations with modern quantum physics. Peat spent one summer in the 1980s attending the Blackfoot Sun Dance ceremony in Alberta, Canada. He engaged in dialogue circles between scientists and Native Elders and wrote about his experiences in *Blackfoot Physics*,

As Above, So Below

in which he compares the myths, stories, traditions, languages, and perceptions of reality between the Western world and the world of the indigenous. What he found were many amazing commonalities in the Blackfoot worldview and the modern world of cutting-edge science and quantum theory. Apparently, one does not need a PhD from an Ivy League university to understand that the macrocosmic and the microcosmic not only work in a similar fashion, but are simply parts of a greater whole, and that we may indeed be just cells in the body of God.

Though Bohm's concepts have received a cool reception in the mainstream physics world, he has become something of a sage to those in the metaphysical community, who find parallels in his work with ancient teachings of oneness, allness, and the eternal and creative source. This vision of wholeness is repeatedly referenced in Buddhist thought, Vedic teachings, Taoism, and even the Western religious traditions that speak of a Kingdom of Heaven—a wholeness in which we all move and have our being. In Huua-yen Buddhism, we hear of the "one to the many" and the "many to the one," as in the flow of source to the manifest world, and the manifest world having its origin in the higher source.

Threes in Technology and Science

Stepping away from the mystical, we would be remiss not to mention other great "threes" in science and technology:

- Three dimensions: width, height, and length.
- Three means of heat transfer: heat connection, heat conduction, and heat convection.
- Three classifications of rocks: igneous, pyroclastic, and sedimentary.
- Three Kepler's laws of orbital movement of planets around the sun: first, each planet's orbit is an ellipse with the sun at one focus; second, the rate of area that is swept by a planet along its orbit is constant; and third, the ration of the semi-major axis to the square of the period is constant for all planets.

The Trinity Secret

- ❀ Three laws of thermodynamics: first law, Conservation of Energy; second law, Entropy; and third law, Entropy as temperature approaches absolute zero.

- ❀ Three laws of motion as per Sir Isaac Newton: first, an object remains at a constant velocity until a non-zero force acts upon it; second, the force will accelerate an object in the direction of that force with the acceleration proportional to the force and inversely proportional to the object's mass; and third, for every force, there is an equal and opposite force.

- ❀ Three states of matter: solid, liquid, and gas.

- ❀ Three hands on a mechanical clock: second, minute, and hour.

- ❀ Three primary colors of light: red, blue, and green.

- ❀ Three primary colors of print: cyan, magenta, and yellow.

- ❀ Three metric measurements: meter, liter, and gram.

- ❀ Three semicircular canals in the human ear.

- ❀ Three sections of the human brain.

- ❀ Three main galaxy morphological classifications: Ellipticals, Spirals, and Lenticulars.

- ❀ DNA and RNA use a triplet codon system.

- ❀ Three parts of an atom: proton, neutron, and electron.

- ❀ Three flavors of quarks in particle physics: charm, strange, and top/bottom.

- ❀ Three quarks in a baryon.

- ❀ Three generations of matter in the Standard Model of fundamental particles.

- ❀ And most importantly, 3 is the channel most of us must have our TV cable box on in order to watch anything!

In earlier chapters we examined the prominence of the triad, and the consistent belief in a threefold process by which we all originated. Add to that the three world levels found in many indigenous traditions,

As Above, So Below

and our own more relatable belief in heaven, earth, and hell, and this concept of three orders of reality becomes more understandable. We spent little time discussing the explicate order of reality, mainly because we all know this order quite well. This is the place where we, as humans, live and move and have our being. We may not quite fully understand what reality is, but we know enough to get us through the days of our lives, accumulating the material goods we need to live and survive and hopefully reproduce. Little do we ever stop to think about how all this material stuff got here, or where it came from. But if what happens "above" is also what happens "below," then it behooves us to understand what we can of these invisible domains, where thought and idea and intention act as the seeds that will one day, in time, grow into something tangible that we can see, feel, hear, smell, or touch.

If the very nature of how matter is made manifest comes from a process of enfoldment and unfoldment in an invisible realm, then by that very act of unfoldment it is made visible to us in our world; the quantum holomovement becomes the God of science, having the same qualities, characteristics, and abilities that are given to deities in religions all over the world. Bohm may have been a mystic as well as a physicist, for surely he saw in the intricate world of quantum behaviors and actions that led him to fully embrace the power of the three. Explicate, implicate, superimplicate.

Creation, creative force, creator. Like the Borromean rings, you simply cannot have one without the others. Remove one of the rings, and the whole thing falls apart.

Syzygy

Syzygy is the alignment of three celestial bodies, such as sun, moon, and earth, when the moon is either full or new. It occurs at either of the two points in the orbit of a celestial body, where the body is in opposition to, or conjunction with, the sun. It can also be the sun, the Earth, and another planet. The word has its root in the Greek *syzygein*, "to yoke together." This conjunction holds meaning for astrologers. In its connection with the calculation of Tide Tables

The Trinity Secret

it applies to the conjunctions and oppositions of sun and moon near the Node. For astronomers, syzygy causes spring tides, because the combined gravitational pull of the moon and sun works together on the Earth's surface. In some cases, conjunction can cause a solar eclipse, when the moon is aligned just right. The study of syzygy can allow astronomers to predict something like an eclipse, making it possible to tell when the eclipse will happen, and where on Earth it will be visible.

It's all about syzygy—alignment—bodies and forces working in conjunction with one another, separate yet whole. Individual yet unified. Just as the Trinity…

7 Ladder of Consciousness: Triple Brain, Triple Mind

Because our entire universe is made up of consciousness, we never really experience the universe directly, we just experience our consciousness of the universe, our perception of it. So right, our only universe is perception.
—Alan Moore

Each of us can manifest the properties of a field of consciousness that transcends space, time, and linear casualty.
—Stanislav Grof

Everything in the Universe, throughout all its kingdoms, is conscious: i.e. endowed with a consciousness of its own kind and on its own plane of perception.
—H.P. Blavatsky

The nature of the Trinity extends into the physical world. Our Universe, our minds, our brains, even our consciousness seem to work on a threefold level. This threefold nature is apparent at both the macrocosmic level of the very, very large, and also at the microcosmic level—our level, the one we exist in every day. It is even there at the quantum level, too. Most of us sense that we are of three minds. Well, if you equate the mind with the brain, that is. We might call those three "primal," "human," and "divine," which would clearly describe the state we might be operating in at any given time. Some of us spend much more time in one of those minds than others. But we all have three minds, and it all begins inside our skulls.

Our brains have a three-part architecture, each with its own unique properties: the forebrain, the midbrain, and the hindbrain. Simple enough. These three parts suggest an evolution from reptile to human, with different roles that afforded us the ability to survive over thousands of years.

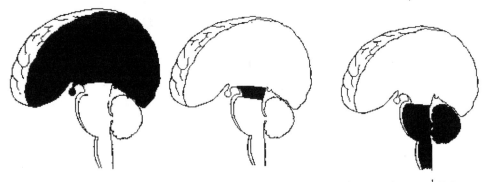

Fig. 7-1, 7-2, and 7-3

The three parts of the human brain.

The hindbrain is the "primitive brain," including the upper part of the spinal cord, the brain stem, and the cerebellum, which looks like a ball of wrinkled-up tissue. The domain of the hindbrain is survival, basic motor skills, posture, and balance, and it controls our breathing, blood pressure, and heart rate—our vital functions necessary for life. The cerebellum coordinates our ability to move and allows us to learn rote movements. The pons and medulla are located in the cerebellum. We often refer to the hindbrain as the "brain stem region." Animals have developed cerebellums, considered the oldest part of the brain in evolutionary terms.

The midbrain is the part of the brain controlling the tectum (the dorsal portion of midbrain) and tegmentum (ventral portion of midbrain). The midbrain is responsible for some of our auditory and visual reflex actions, eye movements, and voluntary movements. We call this section the "mammalian brain." Most of the structure of this part of the brain is shared with even ancient vertebrates, controlling the motivation and habituation of everything from humans to insects. This is also the part of the brain that carries melanin pigment.

The forebrain is the biggest and most highly developed part of the brain, consisting of the cerebrum or cortex and all of the parts hidden by it, including the limbic system (thalamus, hypothalamus, amygdala, and hippocampus) and the four "lobes": the frontal lobe, the parietal lobe, the occipital lobe, and the temporal lobe. We call this part of the brain the "higher brain," for this is the domain of higher functions of thought, action, language, imagination, and reasoning. This section of the brain includes the Broca's area, responsible for our ability to put our thoughts into words. It is also the part of the brain governing emotions.

The bulk of the cerebrum is made up of the neocortex, a six-layered structure found only in mammals, but associated with more fully evolved animals capable of higher thought-processing abilities, such as dolphins, whales, and primates. In terms of evolution, this is the most recently evolved part of the human brain. We know and love it as our "grey matter."

Why Does the Brain Look Like a Wad of Toilet Paper?

There is a reason why the cerebral cortex is so wrinkled in appearance. The wrinkling serves to increase the surface area of the brain, increasing the amount of neurons within, and therefore increasing the brain's efficiency. If we had smoother brains, we wouldn't be as smart!

This is a crash course in the basic structures of the brain, but what is most important is the evolutionary development of the three parts of the brain, necessary as we humans found the need for greater and greater cognitive abilities. The survival mode of the primitive brain led to the more complex abilities of the middle or mammalian brain, leading to the most recent higher brain and its ability to take us beyond sheer survival and rote behavior and into the domains of complex thought processing, perception, and memory.

Triune Brain and the Human Psyche

The three parts of the brain correspond to three parts of the human psyche, which Freud called the id, ego, and superego. Naturally, the development of self-awareness and self-perception would evolve along with the ability of the brain to understand our role within our environment. The reptile brain naturally evolved first, allowing us the gift of instinct, fight-or-flight response, and the desire to claim territory and reproduce. The most rote and basic of emotionssss lives in the reptile brain, the region associated with the id. This is the seat of all human impulse. This is the child brain. It demands satisfaction, and is the domain of impulses, urges, and desires. The child brain throws tantrums and hissy fits, and puts its hands on its hips, demanding "I want it and I want it *now*." It does not reason, has no patience, and clearly does not get the concept of delayed gratification.

The driving force behind the child brain/id is the libido, which Freud described as the instinctual energy and will to survive, the life force. We think of this part of the brain as a child because it acts the way a child does when it wants to be fed or attended to. It demands to be attended to. It is purely survival-based and pure desire—sexual, physical, even emotional at its most base levels. We are born with our id intact, because we need it as newborns to get our basic needs met. We don't care about anyone else's needs yet; the id only cares about its own satisfaction and its own survival.

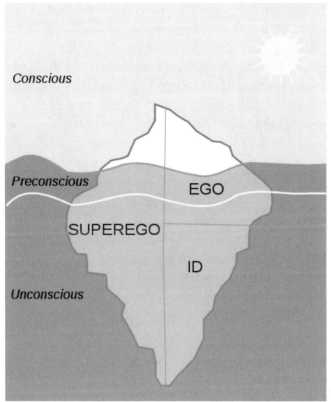

Fig. 7-4

Freud's image of the levels of consciousness, with the greater unconscious below the tip of the iceberg of the conscious.

Although we tend to look down upon these instincts and desires, the child brain/id makes us human. But of course, where you have a child, you must have a parent.

Enter the ego, the domain of the middle brain. The ego acts as a negotiator between the wants and desires of the id and the higher moral brain, or superego. The ego knows that it cannot always get what it wants, and often resists reality, but it also knows that sometimes you have to give a little to get a lot, and acts as a mediator and middleman to take the wild and unruly forces of the id and channel all that hot, crazy energy into reachable goals.

We develop an ego sometime in early childhood, when we start to realize that there is a world out there, and other people in it, and that those other people have their own needs, desires, and ids. The ego teaches us how to make the id happy while also reaching out to others and considering their needs. The ego faces reality—well, part of reality, for even the ego tends to distort reality to its own agenda.

A bit later in childhood, we learn that there is right and wrong. This moral stage of development introduces the superego, the higher brain that judges, and poses moral and ethical restraints upon our behavior. The superego is the conscience and oversees the work of the ego to keep the libido of the id in check. The ego remains, however, the most critical element to the average human life, because the ego is the middle man, again, between the chaotic and uncontrolled impulse of the id and the too-rigid and too-restrained superego.

Well-known theorist Lawrence Kohlberg (1927–1987) developed three stages of moral development that closely correlate Freud's teachings. Kohlberg's work has been widely accepted as applying to the personality development from childhood to adulthood:

1. Preconventional Level—to age 9: Self-Focused Morality—defined as obeying rules to avoid consequences. What satisfies the child's needs is considered good and moral.
2. Conventional Level—age 9 to adolescence: Other-Focused Reality—children begin to comprehend expectations of parents, teachers, peers. Morality is the achievement of these expectations. Children also learn now to fulfill obligations to others.
3. Postconventional Level—adulthood: Higher-Focused Morality—adult understanding of the differing opinions about morality, rules, and laws from group to group. Understanding of one's personal beliefs allows adults to judge their own actions and those of others based upon their own moral code, allowing for independent thought.

Freud's Triune Concepts

Freud took the three-brain/three-psyche concept one step further, developing three levels of consciousness in which the id, ego, and superego did their respective work. The conscious level is our awareness, who we are in the world, although not the entirety of who we truly are. Much of that resides in the second level, the preconscious/subconscious. We have some means of access to what lies in this realm, what is just beyond our consciousness, but so much of it is buried below the surface and often drives our patterns of behavior throughout our lives. This domain is where we store memories, especially those of deep impor- tance, whether positive or traumatic, and the subconscious often has more influence over our conscious beliefs, attitudes, and behaviors than we think, which is why it is often so hard to break a bad habit, or change ourselves on a deep enough level to make it stick. This is also why many people fail at affirmations and the Law of Attraction teachings, because they believe one thing on a conscious level but do not believe it in the subconscious, where it really counts.

The third level, which Freud believed drives most of our emotions, beliefs, and impulses, is the unconscious. This domain is large and is like the iceberg beneath the waters, the tip of which is the small conscious mind and its reality. The vast majority is buried below the surface, and we are often not aware of what lies in the unconscious realm, even though it does show up in our behavior, actions, and beliefs. Whatever experiences in life we have not integrated into our personalities, sit dormant in the unconscious.

A More Scientific Take

A more scientific take comes from theoretical physicist Michio Kaku in his book *Visions: How Science Will Revolutionize the 21st Century*. Kaku writes about the coming age of robotics and quantum physics and the potential for technology to develop such sophisticated robots that they may have some kind of consciousness. Kaku divides consciousness into three levels or degrees:

Ladder of Consciousness

- The lowest level is the ability of an organism to monitor its body and environment. Even an inanimate object like a thermostat could be said to monitor its environment, thus having a type of "consciousness," and that higher up on this degree we would find plants, machines with vision (programmed to recognize patterns in immediate environment), and animals at rest scanning their environment for danger, food, or potential mates.

- The second level includes the entire animal kingdom, marked by the ability to carry out defined goals like survival, reproduction, and the planning associated with such tasks. This is the dominant level of consciousness for human activity. The higher the sophistication of the goal, the higher level of consciousness is required, but we humans spend most of our time at a mid-level of existence, pondering our survival and desire for reproduction, with some fun and play in between.

- The third level is the highest level of consciousness, and allows us to ask and ponder the bigger questions of our existence, our place in the Universe, and how it was all created. This is the level of self-imposed goals that go beyond sheer survival. This is the level of true self-awareness. We aspire to spend more time in this level, but, unfortunately, do not.

Another way to describe the three levels of consciousness are:

- Subconscious—the first level, the repository of memory, experience, belief, and impressions left upon the mind. Could be said to be our own personal field of everything, containing every thought we've ever had.

- Conscious—the normal, everyday waking state of awareness, rational and analytical, problem-solving, and action-oriented.

- Superconscious—the higher mind of intuition and wholeness, does not see the parts, but the whole of a problem or situation. Overseer and uniter.

The superconscious and the superego are aligned with the higher, more evolved brain. The conscious/ego/middle brain then has the ability to take the moral guidance, mercy, forgiveness, and compassion of the superego/higher brain and make it work on a harmonious "earthly level." The ego is the mediator, or peacemaker. The middle brain is the domain of higher order above pure instinct and survival-based response, but not on the level of the higher brain.

The subconscious/id/hindbrain is the home of instinct and is tied into the drive to survive, but also houses the dark recesses of a subconscious that houses old patterns, memories, and behaviors that keep us from accessing the highest level of mind/brain/consciousness.

Huna Teachings and the Three Minds

The Hawaiian Huna teachings, described as an ancient system of wisdom brought into the Western world by Max Freedom Long, who learned of the teachings of Huna from a man named William Tufts Brigham, speak also of three selves or minds. The Huna, the most widely known Hawaiian spiritual tradition, are similar to the secret Egyptian teachings of the Order of Melchizedek, and allow the initiate to access his or her highest level of inner wisdom, using seven principles to bring about healing, harmony, and pure balance of the mind.

The three minds or selves of the Huna teachings parallel the subconscious, conscious, and superconscious mind. The lowest level is the subconscious "Unihipli," or low self. This is the seat of emotion and animal instincts. It is not low in a sense of importance, but rather it is the level below that of normal consciousness.

The middle level is the "Uhane," or middle self. This is the conscious and aware existence of day-to-day life, where we can reason, think, and have free will to create what we please.

The highest level is the "Aumakua," described as the trustworthy parent self of spirit that lives in a higher plane of consciousness outside of the physical body. It does not interfere with our lives unless we desire it to. This is the realm of intuition, dreams, and premonitions that make themselves known via the subconscious. The high self can see into the future as far as your own thoughts are formed, and, as your thoughts change, your future changes as well.

Each of the three Huna levels has its role to play in our lives, and the best result of course is an integration of the three that allows for harmony and balance. Obviously, the same integration is necessary to all of us if we hope to benefit from the best of all three levels of consciousness. When one is out of balance, the other two suffer. Thus, we suffer. The Huna also believe that you can raise your level of consciousness by raising the energy of your vital force, much like modern Law of Attraction teachings tell us we can achieve more success and happiness if we raise our physical and emotional "vibration."

Consciousness and Creation

No matter how you choose to describe the three levels of brain, mind, and consciousness, one thing is clear to many a mystic and scientist alike: The role of consciousness in the creation and perception of reality is profoundly important. In fact, without consciousness, we may not even have a reality to perceive! Noted psychiatrist Stanislov Grof extensively researched the non-ordinary states of human consciousness and found, after 30 years of clinical research and observation, that we are all a part of that "holomovement" David Bohm spoke of. Every one of us, according to Grof, has access to all levels of consciousness. Grof supported much of the research into the holographic model of consciousness, noting in his data a striking amount of phenomenological evidence to support the idea that individual consciousness was like a piece of the collective consciousness, yet contained the whole of the collective within. Grof also believed that the holographic model might explain many of the things we deem paranormal that occur in altered states of consciousness. This could include psychic ability, remote viewing, even seeing into the past or the future, equating the mind as part of a continuum or labyrinth that is connected to every other mind that has ever existed, but also to every atom and organism throughout the Universe. He did not see it as so strange to imagine that the mind might occasionally travel into this labyrinth and experience what he called the "transpersonal."

This corresponds also with the work of Stanford University professor of neuropsychology Karl Pribram and his well-known and extensive studies into the holographic nature of the human brain. One of the key findings of Pribram's research was the strange nature of memory, and how memories might be "enfolded" within every region of the brain, and not localized in particular regions as once thought.

Pribram developed the "holonomic brain theory" in collaboration with Bohm, as a non-conventional model for human cognition. Pribram's inspiration came from the implicate order and how it worked, and the similarity with a hologram, and began to see the same patterns at work in the human brain. Memory and information, Pribram discovered, appear to be distributed throughout the brain, with each "piece" containing the whole memory or informational image. He concluded that there is in the cortex of the brain a "multidimensional holographic-like process serving as an attractor or set point toward which muscular contractions operate to achieve a specified environmental result." This is all based upon the individual's prior experience, and is stored in holographic-like form.

He based his research upon the insights of Dennis Gabor, inventor of the hologram. Gabor's work involved observing the interference patterns of scattering electrons when light strikes them, as in the taking of a photograph. Gabor noticed that there was a method to the madness of the electron scattering, and that is was well regulated. If you then defocused the lens of a camera you could see in the "out-of-focus" blur the hologram itself. This led Pribram to discern that there is a deeper relationship between what we ordinarily experience, and what other process might be going on that is unseen, but in which things are all distributed or spread. He likened this to the implicate order of his colleague, Bohm, and suggested that the types of experiences people have that they label as spiritual may seem to parallel the descriptions of quantum physics. What is going on in the quantum world might in fact mirror what is going on in our own psychological processes and nervous systems, including the brain.

In his fascinating book *The Holographic Universe*, author Michael Talbot looked at how the holographic model of the universe as described by Bohm also applied to the brain, as Pribram's research claimed. Just as the universe seems to act like one giant hologram, so too does the brain. Again: As Above, So Below—all of it pointing to a deeper level of reality where particles are not individual entities, but extensions of the same fundamental "something," and this deeper level of reality connects everything in the universe to everything else. Talbot points to memory storage as only one of the "neurophysiological puzzles" that the holographic theory applies to. The human brain's uncanny ability to retrieve information we need among the enormous storehouse of memories becomes more understandable in light of the hologram theory. Just as in a hologram, Talbot points to how the human thinking process is a perfect example of a "cross-correlated system" in which every piece of information stored in our memory is instantly cross-correlated with every other piece.

"Help Me, Obi Wan..."

Most of us remember that classic scene in *Star Wars* when little R2D2 projects a holographic image of the lovely Princess Leia, pleading for help for her people who were under attack by the evil empire. Now, holograms grace everything from credit cards to jewelry to movie scenes. Basically, a hologram is a 3-D image embedded in a 2-D setting that allows you to see the entire image even if you break it into pieces. Each piece, no matter how small you break it, will contain the image of the whole. Holography was invented in 1947 by Hungarian-British physicist Dennis Gabor while he was attempting to find a method for improving the resolution of electron microscopes. Gabor used a mercury vapor lamp, which produced monochrome blue light, and filters to make his light more coherent. Gabor won the Nobel Prize in physics for his invention in 1971.

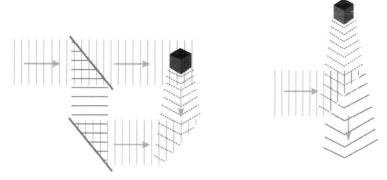

Fig. 7-5   Fig. 7-6

These images show the basic process for recording, and then reconstructing, a holographic image.

Talbot also points to the brain's ability to translate all of the frequencies it receives, including light and sound frequencies, and how it then creates our perceptions from those translations: "Encoding and decoding frequencies is precisely what the hologram does best." He goes on to refer to Pribram's idea of how the brain, like a hologram, functions as a sort of lens, converting the frequencies it receives through the five senses, and then into the "inner world" of our perception. He states that "the concreteness of the world is but a secondary reality and what is 'there' is actually a holographic blur of frequencies."

Lenses, Pribram states, rectify, objectify, and articulate particles. But if you take the lens away, you see the hologram, the distributed whole. He recognized the explicate order we all experience as space/time reality where a tree is a tree and a shoe is a shoe, tied into the implicate, which we experience differently from the physical world. Pribram defined this as the spiritual aspect of our being, but also as a "potential order" that we do not spend much time dwelling in. This potential order is the heart and soul of today's Law of Attraction teachings, and yet is as ancient as humanity itself. Pribram even stated that human potential is based upon the idea that you could reach into the implicate using particular skills to make more of it appear on the explicate level. Creativity might work in the same fashion, starting off in the potential order as a wave form in a distributed system, that then becomes a mental image, at which point, Pribram says, it is pretty much set into the space/time form. All that remains is for it to be made physically manifest.

The Superimplicate Order

This potential order takes us right back to Bohm and his implicate order as the unfoldment and enfoldment of all that is eventually made manifest in the physical world. We might want to associate this implicate order with the Holy Spirit of the Trinity, the activating agent and force by which the explicate world of the Son, or Christ, is made able to walk the Earth. The Father, of course, is the superimplicate, overseeing order. And again, like a hologram, each of the three pieces contains within it the entirety of the whole.

Bohm equated the manifestation of the implicate into the explicate with everything from each atom to every thought and action. In a constant state of unfoldment and enfoldment, consciousness is the tool that drives the process by which the content of the implicate order is made explicate, but also vice versa. That which is explicate then enfolds into even more thought, energy, and action upon the implicate, in an ever-changing, ever-evolving field of potentiality that the consciousness is able to continuously tap into. If we think back to the kingdom of heaven, or the Akasha, or even the Zero Point Field of quantum physics, we see that this generative source of everything continually adds new information based upon the new activity on the physical, manifest level. It's like a nonstop snowball effect, always growing and always generating more and more and more.

Memory may be doing this very same thing—following this very same process of continuous unfoldment and enfoldment—within our own brains. Memory is recorded within the cells of the brain, and continuously built up on by each new thought, action, and experience we have.

The Trinity Secret

Another interesting take on this threefold nature of the mind and consciousness comes from the works of Philip Holder, PhD, Grandmaster of the North American Wing Chun Association. Wing Chun is a style of Kung Fu believed to be more than 200 years old that originated in southern China by a woman named Yim Wing Chun. Legend has it that she learned the art from a Buddhist Nun Ng Mui, or that it may have originated with a group of Shaolin monks. Whatever its true origin, Wing Chun is a simple form of Kung Fu, and considered a jewel among martial arts teachings. It is based upon three empty hand forms and employs a long pole or spear, and Chinese butterfly knives.

Behind what its practitioners say is a deceptively simple appearance, Wing Chun encompasses a storehouse of knowledge. According to Holder, there are three levels of humanity which encompasses the philosophy of Kung Fu. These levels govern human consciousness and behavior.

- Level One—Spontaneous: the highest form of consciousness, dwelling on the present moment, the here and now. The spontaneous mind responds to life as it happens, expecting nothing, not holding on to the past or looking to the future. It is also a state of non-possessiveness that brings freedom, love, and receptiveness.

- Level Two—Calculated: here the mind calculates and manipulates. This is the second level of humanity/consciousness, and it is here the mind uses its version of right and wrong, and steers events accordingly to an end goal, to what it thinks should happen, not necessarily what is.

- Level Three—Imposed: the lowest level of consciousness. This level requires force and wants everything to go along with its plan. This level is also punishing of what does not go along. This is the realm of control, of people, and of events, bringing little satisfaction, short-term or long-term. Totally task-oriented.

Ladder of Consciousness

Ties to the Trinity

Holder's descriptions of these three levels closely correspond with everything else we have discussed in this chapter. Whether we are referring to Bohm's three levels of order, Freud's three levels of the psyche, or the three parts of the human brain, it is impossible not to see the obvious. Each of the three easily corresponds to an aspect of the Trinity that may or may not have been understood on a conscious level by those who, thousands of years ago, sought to figure out the relationship of the three parts to the whole. The highest level is always the level of the Divine, of God, of the Father. Even for those not of a religious bent, we see how the highest levels of the brain, consciousness, and reality function as the superior overseer, watching the activities of the two levels below it, guiding and directing from its perspective of the "bigger picture," seeing the wholeness and unity of all the parts.

The middle level is the realm of the implicate and invisible, the field of all possibilities upon which we place our orders for how we want reality to show up in the physical world. This is the realm of the Holy Spirit, the processing of unfolding and enfolding, and taking the ideas, desires, and intentions of the highest level and molding, shaping, and forming them for revelation in the lowest level.

The lowest level is where we are as we write this book, or where you are as you read it. The Son represents that which is made manifest in the physical world. If we look to the Christian interpretation of the Trinity, we see how Christ was the spirit of God made visible. Christ was the Divine in human form, and appeared in the explicate level of reality to be seen, heard, and learned from. His teachings would have been pointless had He remained in the domain of the higher levels. He needed to "come down to earth" to make His presence known. Here in this level, we operate mostly on instinct and our need to survive and reproduce, but we have access to the middle level and the highest level if we choose. We can transcend and rise from the limitations of our physical body to the worlds of higher thought, mind, and consciousness.

And, just as the hologram is a whole, and each piece contains the image of the whole, we each contain the whole of this entire process of creation within us, just as we are a part of creation. The same process by which we were made manifest allows us to make manifest. Like the Kung Fu art of Wing Chun, it is hugely complex—and yet deceptively simple.

Was this tri-fold nature of everything intuited by ancient civilizations? Do we still, on some level, intuit this same nature today? If you look at the hugely popular Law of Attraction teachings and the mega-selling *The Secret* as any indication, the answer is a resounding "yes." But before we show you how, there is one level of the Trinity that is of particular importance, and deserves its day in the sun. You cannot see it, but you can see its effects all around you.

Yeast of Fire,
Breath of Life

Inhale, and God approaches you. Hold the inhalation, and God remains with you. Exhale, and you approach God. Hold the exhalation, and surrender to God.
—Krishnamacharya

For breath is life, and if you breathe well you will live long on earth.
—Sanskrit proverb

May the Force be with you.
—Obi-Wan Kenobe

We are the living links in a life force that moves and plays around and through us, binding the deepest soils with the farthest stars.
—Alan Chadwick

The Trinity is made up of three parts, but to most people who have a general understanding of it, the middle aspect, or the Holy Spirit, is the one they have the most trouble with. What is this spirit? Is it exclusive to Christian teachings? What does it have to do with a process or code of creation? Think about the last time you baked bread. If you ever did, that is, for nowadays it's far too easy to get it already baked. But let's imagine what is necessary for the process. We have the basic ingredients of flour and water, and our end goal is a warm, crusty loaf of bread. But without one extra ingredient, we can never get the gooey dough that the flour and water make into a form that will be edible once it's done.

We need to make the dough rise. And for that, we need yeast.

Going back to the traditional Trinity, as Jesus said in the Gospel of St. John, "The Father and I are one" (John 10:30). But how are they one? What is the secret ingredient—the missing link between the physical world of the man on earth, and the divine world of the transcendent, Cosmic One? What is the second part of the process by which the implicate idea of something becomes physical in the explicate order? Can't it just appear?

To get something out of nothing, you need to do something. There must be an action, or an activating agent, by which the no thing becomes some thing. The Holy Spirit thus becomes the most important part of the Trinity, for one who understands and recognizes what this element stands for, understands the process of creation itself.

Why Yeast?

If you've ever wondered why yeast is such an important ingredient in making dough rise and become a delicious pizza crust or loaf of bread, it is all chemical. Flour is the structure of the bread, providing the starch and protein, which will combine to form the elastic protein, gluten. Add in water and stir, and you get the stretchy dough that, when kneaded over and over, creates a sheet of gluten that can be filled with gas, forming bubbles that will make the texture of the bread lighter. The yeast is what supplies the gas, feeding on sugars in the flour, and producing carbon dioxide gas and ethyl alcohol. Salt can be added to slow down the fermentation rate and ensure a desired texture. And to break up small clusters or colonies of yeast cells so they come into contact with more sugars and air, you "punch down" the dough the first time it rises and let it rise again for a shorter period. Different types of flour give the yeast more nutrients, primarily sugars, to work with, resulting in a different flavor. Interestingly, that most delicious of sourdough breads, San Francisco Sourdough, can *only* be made in San Francisco! The special bacteria in the bread is original to the area, and a wild yeast that is native to the area as well is the only type of yeast that will grow with this special bacteria! But don't stress: You can buy a complete mix at the store and enjoy San Francisco Sourdough even if you live in Cleveland.

The Holy Spirit as Divine Essence

Spirit has always been understood as having no physical nature. Invisible. The Holy Spirit of the Judeo-Christian tradition is likened to a divine breath or fire of the spirit that is either poured upon the body or given to others from the body as if being poured out. It is also described as a "fullness," as in Ephesians 3:19, "the fullness of God," or Ephesians 4:13, "the fullness of Christ." Deities were said to be filled with a Divine "essence," something we lowly humans could only aspire to, or have gifted upon us if a God or Goddess saw fit. Job 33:4 even refers to the breath of the almighty.

But we can look at our own bodies and know that the same essence flows through us, as the breath that keeps us alive and gives us the animating life force. It is the part of us we recognize as giving our minds and bodies a means of expression and individuality. Without the spirit element, we are like zombies, with a basic functioning survival-based brain pushing our bodies along. Lifeless.

Some might equate the Holy Spirit with the soul, which is independent of the body, and can enter and leave the body upon birth and death. The ancient Egyptians had a unique three-part perspective of existence similar to the trikaya of Tibetan Buddhism. These three parts all served some role in animating us as living, breathing beings. In his *Death, Burial and Afterlife in Ancient Egypt*, author James Romano discusses the "ka," "ba," and "khu" as three separate yet similar aspects of the soul. The "ka" is the one that most equates with the Holy Spirit, for this is the vital essence or vital force of an individual, represented in images as two upraised arms.

Fig. 8-1

A ka-statue from ancient Egypt. The ka is said to dwell within the statue.

Ka was created when a person was born, and those of a royal nature could have more than one ka. The ka stayed separate from the physical body, so when someone died he or she returned to the ka. The ka was said to dwell within mummies or tomb statues, called ka-statues. The ka could also be equated with today's "psyche," and was once associated with ghosts of the dead. For the ka to continue on after death, the deceased's family would make offerings in the tomb. The ka was said to travel between the world of the living and its own world of existence via "false doors," which were funerary stelae covered with magical formulas.

Ka is what basically distinguished the living from the dead.

The "ba" is equally interesting, for this is the animating part of the spirit that was free to leave the tomb and move about the earth during the day, returning to the tomb at night. Often depicted as a human-headed bird, the ba was said to leave the body at death, but could return to the tomb to reanimate the dead. The ba is often referred to as the "soul," "spirit," or "spiritual manifestation," and even animals were said to be the bau (plural of ba) of specific deities. Today the ba is considered the closest thing in nature to our contemporary understanding of the soul, but is also related to personality and what makes each of us unique.

The "khu" was associated with intelligence, but also meant spirit, as the khu of the Gods resided in heaven. Upon death, human khu could also enter heaven if prayed for.

To the ancient Aramaic, the *Rhua d'Qoodsha* (Holy Breath) served as the Source of Breath for all life on the planet. This is not the first, or only, time that the Holy Spirit has been described in terms of breath. The Kabbalah describes the Divine Breath, the life force with which all things were created: "So God, great and mighty, and awesome, powerfully breathed out a breath, and cosmic space expanded to the boundary determined by divine wisdom, until God said, 'Enough!'" This life force is the Holy Spirit "coursing the pathways of existence, through all desires, all worlds, all thoughts, all nations, all creatures."

Just as the Universe was created by the breath of the life force blown from the lungs of God, the process is repeated in our own search for unification with the creative life force. By embracing the Holy Spirit, we become one with God. By the very breath that courses through our being, we are one with God already.

The vital force or divine essence, the holy breath and spirit of life, the life energy and soul. Here are a sampling of terms used by cultures and traditions around the world to describe this activating and animating agent:

Ha—the Polynesian "life force" uniting the soul, or uhane, with the body.

Elan vital—the principal energy of creation according to French philosopher Henri Bergson.

Semangat—a Malaysian word for the life force that exists not only in plants, animals, and people, but in some places and objects as well.

Spiritus Animalis—Latin word for "soul spirit" and refers to the Greek "pneuma psychikon."

Anima Mundi—the "world soul" of Plato described in his book *Timaeus*.

Akwalu—the spiritual light or essence of the Akawaio Indians of Guyana.

Baraka—the breath of God in sufism, a mystical movement of Islam.

Boha—the force or power throughout all of nature to the Shoshon Indian tribe.

Mana—the Polynesian divine force.

Manitou—the spiritual force or life force behind all things in nature, including humans, according to the Algonquin Indian tribe.

Ni—the life force of the Oglala Indians.

Po-wa-ha—the Pueblo Indian term for the creative spirit flowing through nature.

Digi—Apache Indian for the force that permeates nature.

Ki—the Japanese form of the Chinese qi, or life force.

Kra/okra—the soul force of the Akan tribe of Africa.

Ankh—an older Egyptian term for life spirit.

Kurunba—the Australian Aborigine word for life force or spirit that permeates a place. The Aborigine also referred to "miwi" as soul or spirit.

Orgone energy—life energy, according to the work of Swiss psychologist Wilhelm Reich, a student of Freud. This was the primordial energy of the universe, the cosmic energy.

Tondi—the word for animating life force of the Batak people of Indonesia.

And, our favorite...

The Force—George Lucas used the term in his *Star Wars* films to describe the neutral life force or universal energy accessible to the Jedi. But we can all use the Force. How we choose to use it is up to us!

The Buddhist Way

Buddhists understand that the way to enlightenment is a process by which an ordinary man becomes a mystic through meditation and breath work. Thus, the Holy Spirit can be described as the means to an end, the end being Divine Union. The means can be many things: meditation and contemplation, breath work, yogic poses, service to others, love. Any action that allows for the further expansion of consciousness can be considered a powerful activating agent like the Holy Spirit. Buddhists focus especially on "mindfulness" to achieve this state of unified being.

Buddhists like Thich Nhat Hanh believe that it is in these moments of complete oneness with the present moment that we find God, or "the Buddha within ourselves who transcends space and time." Jesus and Buddha are perfect examples of ordinary men who used the key of the Holy Spirit in order to achieve the Kingdom of God within. Whether by the prayer of a Christian or the meditation of a Buddhist (prayer is meditation, meditation is prayer), the consciousness must be opened to the Spirit in order to be one with the Spirit itself.

Buddhists express the expansion of the ordinary mind into enlightenment of Nirvana via the Three Buddha Bodies; those of Truth, Reality, and Beauty. But a paradox is raised here. For in the absolute sense, the three bodies really can only be one, as all three bodies are found within the one united whole, as indicated here in Padma Sambhava's teaching in the Tibetan Book of the Dead, where Padma describes the Detailed Identification of infinite intelligence:

This objective identification of the actuality of things contains complete in one the indivisible Three Bodies.
The Truth Body, the voidness free of intrinsic status,
The Beatific Body, bright with freedom's natural energy,
The Emanation Body ceaselessly arising everywhere-
Its reality is these three complete in one.

There is only one Buddha, just as there is only one God. Yet, there are countless Buddhas and countless Gods as each person who perfects Divine Union becomes a Buddha or God (the microcosm of the macrocosm). Perhaps this paradox most confused early Christians striving to understand how God could be separate from the Son, yet the Son could be one with God.

Via the activating agent, the Holy Spirit, or yeast of fire, man is filled with the very presence of God. Yet the Holy Spirit is *not* God! This confusion becomes a little clearer when we understand the Unity School of Christianity teaching that the Holy Spirit is the whole activity of God moving through the hearts and minds of people. This stance adopts a more active position for the Holy Spirit, again like yeast in bread dough that corresponds with the "procreative *pneuma*" or "ministering wind" from the Isis mysteries and the Helios apotheosis respectively. The Helios apotheosis specifically associates the ministering wind as the breath streaming from the sun God into the soul in order to fructify it. Later in Christianity, this fructifying agent is represented as a dove, the symbol for the Holy Spirit or Ghost that "impregnated" Mary and "descended upon" Saul on the road to Damascus, causing his great conversion.

Other Names for the Holy Spirit

The Chinese *chi* concept of energy pervading all things can be correlated with the Holy Spirit. Chi exists in and all around us, the Vital Breath. In Hindu it is *prana*, in Hebrew tradition it is *ruah*. In Greek it is *pneuma*, and in Latin it is *spiritus*. But it is all the same: the life-giving breath of God. The chi in Taoist thought represents the "thread" between the *Tao*, the Universal Soul, and the *Te*, the personal soul. This is also apparent in the Indian notion of the *sutra* (thread) being the link between *atman*, the individual soul, and *Brahman*, universal soul. The word *sutra* has been given many originations, but many scholars believe it derives from the root *siv*, which means to stitch together, as in the English "suture." This is an obvious example of a very simple path to enlightenment, with the personal joining the universal via a threadlike link often referred to as "energy" or "life-giving breath."

Modern students of most Eastern traditions understand that, in order to reach a state of being that is transcendent, one must "do something," such as devotion, contemplation, meditation, chanting, or, in some cases, suffering. This corresponds to the belief Christians hold that prayer and devotion lead to union with God. This also applies to the act of creation: You cannot just speak something into being. There must be a mechanism by which the word becomes form, a vibrational resonance or frequency, an invisible movement of etheric energy, a force beyond the five senses that organizes the non-order and chaos into order, substance, and form. This mechanism, like the breath in our lungs, gives "life" to that which had no life, no form. Thus, perhaps union with the divine really is another way to describe the act of creation. When we are in the oneness, the implicate, the Force, or the Akasha, we are immersed in the very energies and forces and potentialities that will, if we desire, become our created reality.

Christian Concepts of Divine Union

To this day, Christianity holds two schools of thought when it comes to union with the divine. One school, the school of Church Fathers and dogma and doctrine, still holds fast to the rule that God can only be accessed via another higher-evolved human being (pope, bishop, priest) who alone knows the way to God. The other school believes that the way Jesus spoke of is applicable and accessible to us all, and that all that is required are service, devotion, and prayer. St. Paul called it "praying without ceasing," and Jesus himself suggested that in seeking the Kingdom of God first, everything else would be added on top of it, insinuating that the Kingdom was inherent in everyone, as were all the blessings and riches it contained. In a purely scientific sense, this Holy Spirit or activating breath must be available to us all, if we are indeed immersed in it! Thus no middle man was or is needed to become the creators using the creative forces to create. We are the middle men.

In ancient Greek terminology, the Holy Spirit was referred to as "*pneuma*," which is a genderless term. The word, meaning "spirit" or "breath," indicates that, in order to access union with God, we must first be filled with something else, this breath or spirit. Early Christians thought this breath would fill us from outside us, but Gnostics and mystics understood that the spirit was already within us, and that all we had to do was realize this truth, and we would be set free. By constantly looking outside of oneself for the Holy Spirit, we miss the very presence of it within us already. Thus, in the early days of the Church, only people who had visible, ecstatic, "rapturous" experiences were said to have been touched by the Holy Spirit, thus excluding the rest of the populated world as unchosen and unlucky!

Religious Science founder Ernest Holmes presented the world with a metaphysical concept of spiritual mind treatment, a type of affirmative prayer that served to unite a person with his or her divine essence via "recognition" of that very consciousness within. To Holmes and other founders of New Thought religions such as Unity, Divine Science, Spiritual Science, and Christian Science, there was no separation—*never* any separation between the Father and the Son. The only separation was the lack of "recognition" or "realization" of this oneness in consciousness. Thus the motto of Religious Science, "Change Your Thinking, Change Your Life," came to mean that by opening one's conscious mind to accept and be aware of the divine essence within, one would become unified with that divine essence.

In other words, by becoming conscious of our oneness with divinity, we become one with divinity. By focusing our consciousness on God, we become God.

Consciousness, then, is everything.

Christian Scientists use this unification with the perfect divine essence as the basis for their powerful belief that healing occurs through the denial of separation from the perfection of the Divine. By affirming union with God, healing occurs, for God knows no dis-ease. All of the work, all of the healing, is done in the realm of consciousness. This is the realm of the Holy Spirit. Holmes likens the threefold nature of the

Universal Being as "…spirit as the great actor, Soul as the medium of its action, and Body as the result of its action." One power alone is really acting, but in a threefold process involving the levels of body, mind (soul), and spirit.

Plotinus suggested that Nature creates itself through contemplation. Perhaps contemplation, prayer, meditation, breath work, and other processes that quiet the mind and open our consciousness to union with the Divine are the agents by which we create our own lives. Perhaps we work as co-creators with the Life Force, filling ourselves with the Holy Breath that gives us that same life force—that same creative power. Although Buddhists meditate to lift the mind to spiritual heights of enlightenment, Christians and Jews pray and offer devotion to feel the loving essence of God at work in their lives, and monks chant, fast, and practice abstinence to achieve a purified state of being.

Of Fields and Forces

Amazingly, all the most cutting-edge discoveries in quantum physics we discussed earlier, including the potential of the Zero Point Field as a field of intention where thought is impressed upon and then manifested in the material world, give even more credence to the idea that we co-create our reality along with God, or the Life Force. Even more stunning is that this "Force," made famous in the *Star Wars* movies, is totally neutral and that we alone decide how we will use it—for good or for evil (just like Obi-Wan Kenobi said!). Our conscious intention is the yeast of fire that fuels the creative process, and, as Bell's Theorem states, there is an invisible and unbroken bond between all things, and something done to one thing is done to everything else. If this isn't absolute scientific proof that "Do Unto Others" is the ultimate Golden Rule, we'd be hard pressed to say what is.

The idea of a neutral force, or even a neutral God, does not sit well with the followers of the world's great religions, who want their concept of the Divine to prevail. How can evil exist, though, unless this force is indeed neutral, for if it is not neutral, then God has a lot of explaining to do. The neutrality of the creative force allows for anything and everything to be made manifest. We can make good, and evil. We can kill, and cure. We can create, and destroy. The force by which we do so cares not why we do it. It will make whatever we ask it to.

Christian Scientists use denials and affirmations to heal; yogis use breath work and body postures to raise their consciousness; shamans induce trance states to travel among the realms of the Lower World, Middle World, and Upper World; Wiccans use the alpha state to achieve union with the Life Force of nature; mystics enter rapturous states of ecstasy through prayer; Dervishes whirl their way to oneness; Muslims bow in ecstatic prayer to *ah-Lah*; we are all in search of the way, the path, the technique to spiritual union with the force of all creation. And yet we need not search, for the way is clear, via the Trinity and all that it symbolizes in every religion, that the only thing standing between God and Man is the Holy Spirit, the breath of life itself, which can be accessed at any time by any one.

"Because God the Son is made of the energy of the Holy Spirit, He is the door for us to enter the Kingdom of God," Thich Nhat Hanh reminds us. "The only place we can touch Jesus and the Kingdom of God is within us." The same goes for Buddhists, where life gives us the opportunity in each moment to "breathe life into the Buddha, Dharma, and the Sangha. Every moment is an opportunity to manifest the Father, the Son and the Holy Spirit." Were it not in our power to manifest the Trinity, there would be no Trinity. For every great symbol is born of a reality that is present in the consciousness of all.

Thus, the physical Trinity, the archetypal Trinity, and the Trinity process are in and of themselves a Trinity, a threefold nature of Man, God, and the path to God. And again, the very process of creation itself.

The Secret Within Us

Creator. Creation. Act of Creating. The holy spirit or breath of life, the vital force, the essence and fire of existence, is the power behind the act of creation—that which makes the living alive. This breath, like the breath we take to fill our lungs with life-giving oxygen, is what fuels the fire of creation itself. It is the yeast that causes the ingredients to become bread. Its home is in the implicate order. We cannot see it. But we can see its results all around us, even in ourselves. Everything we are, everything we see around us, and touch and smell and hear and taste—all are a result of the yeast we put into the flour and water of creation and bring forth our own "daily bread." "Give us this day our daily bread" takes on a whole new meaning when looked at in terms of our own position in this powerful code of creation. Are we the Father, the Son, or the Holy Spirit? Are we all three at once? And if so, doesn't that make us Godlike? There—we've said it. If we equate God with creator, then the Trinity Secret tells us that we too are capable of the divine act of creating.

But a secret revealed holds no power unless it can be used as a tool for transformation. If we understand that the Trinity really is the process of creation and the path to oneness with the Divine, and that we must access the path via the activation of the Holy Spirit within, then how do we ultimately use the Trinity Secret to activate it? It matters very little if you understand the formula for creation. Until you understand your own role in that formula, and how you can use it, and *do* use it every single day of your life, it means nothing.

If the Holy Spirit is indeed the key to the inner kingdom by which we create our outer kingdom, we need to ask ourselves another question:

Where is the door?

This leads to another question:

What do we do once we open it?

In the next chapter, we will find out.

Yeast of Fire, Breath of Life

9 Keys to the Kingdom: The Secret Revealed

I know that's a secret, for it's whispered everywhere.
—William Congreve

Nothing is as difficult to see as the obvious.
—Bronislaw Malinowski, A Scientific Theory of Culture

Imagination is the beginning of creation. You imagine what you desire, you will what you imagine and at least you create what you will.
—George Bernard Shaw

Creator. Creation. Creative Force.

Father. Son. Holy Spirit.

That's it. That's the code, the secret, the key. Before you close the book in disgust and disappointment over the ridiculous simplicity of it all, be warned: It isn't as simple as it looks. In fact, few people have ever been able to truly master this secret at all. And we wonder why so many of us get more of what we don't want than what we do want? Because, just as this secret works on a cosmic level, with God or source or whatever you wish to refer to the Father aspect as using the forces of natural laws to create the entirety of the universe, *we do the same in our individual lives.* Most of us don't even know nor comprehend our role in the creation of the physical realities we exist in. If only. Yet people have been trying to tell us this "secret" for thousands of years, most recently with a little book that took the world by storm.

In 2006, a little film called *The Secret* was released by Prime Time Productions. The theme of the film, which consisted of interviews and commentary by enlightened leaders and thinkers, was that you could think something into existence. Basically, whatever you wanted could be easily made manifest merely by thinking about it. That there was indeed a Law of Attraction that gives us everything we want, whether it is good or bad or in between.

The film was released online and in DVD format only. Rhonda Byrne was inspired to do the film after reading *The Science of Getting Rich* by Wallace D. Wattles, a book that was published in 1906. Byrne put the project together for Channel Nine in Australia, shooting a series of interviews during 2005 with entrepreneurs, spiritual teachers, authors, scientists, and luminaries in the field of human empowerment. The film was followed up by a book version, written by Byrne, that exploded overnight in sales as people devoured the possibility that they could change their lives by changing their thoughts.

As book sales climbed, Byrne's work was featured all over the media, including appearances with Oprah Winfrey, Ellen DeGeneres, and Larry King, as well as every mainstream media outlet out there. As the book continued to gain exposure and publicity the critics came out of the closet, blood dripping from their fangs, eager for Byrne's blood. They proceeded to tear her, and her work, to pieces as commercial fluff, positive-thinking mumbo jumbo solely designed to make her a millionaire by playing on people's "get-rich-quick-and-easy" desires. Little did they know that the material in the book had its basis in teachings from thousands of years ago, as well as the more recent spiritual concepts presented by the New Thought movement of the 19th century.

Millions of people who purchased the book or the DVD tried the formula presented within—the actual "secret"—and then bitched, moaned, and complained when they failed to materialize great wealth, a new house, or a better-looking spouse. They whined to the media that they did their affirmations, thought positive, and were *still* miserable. Byrne took the brunt of the criticisms, with people cruelly calling her a fake, fraud, and everything in between.

The problem is that the teachings in the book were absolutely correct. The film was spot on. Byrne was doing the world a huge favor, but the world wasn't willing to do the hard work that it required. The "secret" works. Ask. Believe. Receive. The people who were working it just didn't know how it worked! This secret is not new, and certainly not a result of the "new age" movement. This secret has been around for thousands of years, and has been spoken and taught by wise sages and religious leaders, including Hermes, Jesus, and Lao Tzu, and guess what?

It is the very same secret as the Trinity Secret. Too bold a statement? Remember: All wisdom and knowledge are as old as time itself, just waiting for those of us who have the willingness to tap into it. So where Byrne's groundbreaking book left off, other books on the Law of Attraction quickly stepped in to fill in the blanks. Now we offer up a connection as old as time itself—a connection between the Trinity and the secret of all secrets. Let's go back in time and see where the secret began, and why it so often takes on the threefold form of the Trinity.

Primitive Sympathetic Magic

We have no written record of the most primitive of cultures, other than cave art images and crude attempts at visual communication. Yet even here we might see the gleaning of wisdom. Primitive people understood that in order to find animals to eat, you had to think like them—become them. By drawing images of humans morphed into these animals, you acquired some of their power, their essence. You could then think like the animals thought, and know where the animals would go, so you could hunt them down and eat them. You wanted to eat. You found a way to believe you could eat. You got to eat. Ask. Believe. Receive. This is what ancient rites and rituals were all about: putting people in the mindset to put out into the universe what they wanted, and getting the result, whether it is rain, a healing, or even a complete transformation. Though the manner by which they asked the Universe for what they wanted—say, animal and human sacrifice—was questionable, the point is, they had a desire, they took an action, and they got a result (not always the result they really wanted, but we will talk about that later).

Leaping ahead to ancient religious and spiritual teachings, we have, as mentioned in an earlier chapter, the Thrice-Great Hermes and his approximately 5,000-year-old sacred writings. The *Hermetica* tells us that God is Big Mind, and that all that exists are but thoughts in the mind of God made manifest in the Cosmos. Interestingly enough, both Einstein and Stephen Hawking, two of the greatest scientists ever known, believe that the goal of modern science is to "know the mind of God." In *The Hermetica: The Lost Wisdom of the Pharaohs*, authors Timothy Freke and Peter Gandy discuss Hermes' initiation into the secrets of creation of the universe itself.

Via a mystical vision, Hermes perceives something very much like the Big Bang of modern scientific theory. He sees an all-embracing Divine Light, which he equates with the Mind of God. This Light is cast over the dark, restless water, which represents the unlimited potential from which God fashions the Universe (implicate order). There is a vast explosion of light upon the water, much like the Big Bang's explosion of light and energy and eventually matter and form. From the turbulent depths of the dark waters, Hermes hears a cry of suffering. Then he hears the Light speak a Word (Logos), calming the chaos into order. "This Word is like a blueprint that will organize a structured cosmos out of chaos," the authors continue, equating this with the fundamental laws of nature.

But Word is the first thought from the Mind of God set out upon the unlimited potential of the dark waters to create the manifest Universe. Father—Mind of God. Son—Manifest Universe.

The Word—Holy Spirit.

In an interesting twist, Hermes equated the Son with the Word, and we do see this in many religions (Logos as the Son in manifest form), but the process by which that manifestation occurs is always the same: always the "middle man" of the Trinity—the activating agent. From *The Hermetica*:

The Trinity Secret

My Guide asked:
"Do you understand the secrets of this vision?
I am that Light—the Mind of God,
Which exists before
The chaotic dark waters of potentiality.
My calming Word is the Son of God—
The idea of beautiful order,
The harmony of all things with all things."

Hermes is then told by his Guide that the human mind gives birth to speech, and that they cannot be divided one from the other, for "life is the union of Mind and Word." Again, in this context, the Word becomes the activating agent by which God or Mind of God brings forth life. The Light, or Mind of God, continues to form the infinite, ordered world, based upon "the boundless primal idea, which is before the beginning. By Atum's (God's) will, the elements of nature were born as reflections of this primal thought in the waters of potentiality."

Word. Will. Thought.

Atum is everywhere
Mind cannot be enclosed
Because everything exists within Mind.
Nothing is so quick and powerful.
Just look at your own experience.
Imagine yourself in any foreign land,
And quick as your intention,
You will be there!

Word. Will. Thought. Intention.

All things are thoughts,
which the Creator thinks.

That is the secret. Can you see it now?

Keys to the Kingdom

That which IS is manifested;
  That which has been or shall be, is unmanifested, but not dead.
  For soul, the eternal activity of God, animates all things.

Wow. God, then the physical manifested, and the eternal activity that animates all things. Father, Son, Holy Spirit.

In the Hindu tradition, there is a timeless story about a truth seeker who meets with a renowned saint, asking with reverence for the saint to impart his knowledge and teachings. The saint then says three words that sum up the entirety of the teachings. *Three words.* "Tat tvam asi," or "Thou art that." Three simple words that fully describe all the truth seeker needs to know. The indwelling God. Hindus believe that God dwells in all matter, but that matter is not God. God and matter are "coextensive" and the physical world is but a veil of illusions that conceal an underlying hidden reality. Explicate hiding the implicate. These three words are also similar to "I am that." Incredibly, this is simply another way of saying "I am both the creator and the creation itself."

In the Tao, the writings of the ancient Chinese sage Chuang Tzu, the Tao or the Way is everything, the "I am" of creation out of which "is-ness" comes forth:

This is the Great Tao
  it has both reality and substance, but it does nothing
  and has no material form.
  A teacher can transmit it
  But can't guarantee its perception.
  It can be found, but it can't be seen:
  It is its own source, its own root.
  Before there was heaven and earth,
  From of old, there is was,
  Eternally existing.

From this Great Tao, all of existence came, including that of spirit and of God. Chuang Tzu describes Tao as having no beginning or end, and that it cannot be heard, or seen. It simply fills heaven and Earth, and all that is within the universe is enveloped in it. The Tao is the limit of the unlimited and produces all fullness and emptiness, yet is neither full nor empty. It gathers together, and it disperses, but it itself is neither gathered nor dispersed.

The Tao and the Field

If this sounds a lot like the enfolding and unfolding implicate order, or the grand, ground self-regenerating Zero Point Field, surprise! It is. Amazingly, even our own more widely known Western religious traditions understood this unseen realm through which form and substance arose. In the New Testament of the Bible, Christ speaks of the kingdom of heaven in similar terms, as being within and around, yet not seen. Christ also referred to his teachings as the way, and that through the truth he taught one could come to the light, so to speak. And if we look at some of the things Christ taught, they sound an awful lot like rules for using the Law of Attraction.

Mark 11:23 For verily I say unto you, That whosoever shall say unto this mountain, Be thou removed, and be thou cast into the sea; and shall not doubt in his heart, but shall believe that those things which he saith shall come to pass; he shall have whatsoever he saith.

Mark 11:24 Therefore I say unto you, What things soever ye desire, when ye pray, believe that ye receive them, and ye shall have them.

Matthew 21:22 And all things, whatsoever ye shall ask in prayer, believing, ye shall receive.

Matthew 9:28–30 And when he was come into the house, the blind men came to him: and Jesus saith unto them, Believe ye that I am able to do this? They said unto him, Yea, Lord. Then touched he their eyes, saying, According to your faith be it unto you. And their eyes were opened; and Jesus straitly charged them, saying, See that no man know it.

Keys to the Kingdom

Mark 9:23 Jesus said unto him, If thou canst believe, all things are possible to him that believeth.

Matthew 7:7 Ask, and it shall be given you; seek, and ye shall find; knock, and it shall be opened unto you.

Job 22:28 Thou shalt also decree a thing, and it shall be established unto thee: and the light shall shine upon thy ways.

Mark 10:52 And Jesus said unto him, Go thy way; thy faith hath made thee whole. And immediately he received his sight, and followed Jesus in the way.

Matthew 18:19 Again I say unto you, That if two of you shall agree on earth as touching any thing that they shall ask, it shall be done for them of my Father which is in heaven.

In the words of Buddha we see the same concepts.

We are what we think. All that we are arises with our thoughts. With our thoughts, we make our world.

All that we are is the result of what we have thought. If a man speaks or acts with an evil thought, pain follows him. If a man speaks or acts with a pure thought, happiness follows him, like a shadow that never leaves him.

All things appear and disappear because of the concurrence of causes and conditions. Nothing ever exists entirely alone; everything is in relation to everything else.

The Trinity Secret

From the Kabbalah:

Three are the dwellings of the sons and daughters of Man. Thought, feeling and body. When the three become one, you will say to this mountain "move" and the mountain will move.

When the three becomes one. Sound familiar?

They Said It, Too!

The idea that we are a part of the process of creation is not new, and has been credited with the successes of some very amazing people.

Henry Ford—*Whether you think you can or can't either way you are right.*

Alexander Graham Bell—*What power this is I cannot say. All that I know is that it exists.*

Winston Churchill—*You create your own universe as you go along.*

Albert Einstein—*Imagination is everything. It is the preview of life's coming attractions.*

William James—*The greatest discovery of my generation is that human beings can alter their lives by altering their attitudes of mind.*

Ernest Holmes—*Change your thoughts, change your life.*

Napoleon Hill—*Whatever your mind can conceive and can believe, it can achieve.*

Joseph Campbell—*Follow your bliss, and doors will open for you that you never knew existed. Follow your bliss and the universe will open doors for you where there were only walls.*

Wayne Dyer—*I will see it when I believe it.*

Carl Jung—*What you resist persists.*

Keys to the Kingdom

Robert Collier—*All power is from within and is therefore under our control.*

Max Planck—*All matter originates and exists only by virtue of a force... We must assume behind this force the existence of a conscious and intelligent Mind. This Mind is the matrix of all matter.*

Marcus Aurelius—*Our life is what our thoughts make it.*

James Allen—*Let a person radically alter his thoughts and he will be astonished at the rapid transformation it will effect in the material conditions of his life.*

Benjamin Disraeli—*Nurture your mind with great thoughts for you will never go higher than you think.*

Richard Bach—*You are never given a wish without also being given the power to make it true. You may have to work at it, however.*

Andrew Carnegie—*I am no longer cursed by poverty because I took possession of my own mind, and that mind has yielded me every material thing I want, and much more than I need. But this power of mind is a universal one, available to the humblest person as it is to the greatest.*

Gary Zukav—*By choosing your thoughts, and by selecting which emotional currents you will release and which you will reinforce, you determine the quality of your Light. You determine the effects that you will have upon others, and the nature of the experiences of your life.*

Walt Disney—*If you can dream it, you can do it.*

Anatole France—*To accomplish great things we must not only act, but also dream, not only plan but also believe.*

Lao Tzu—*If you correct your mind, the rest of your life will fall into place.*

The New Thought Movement

Moving forward a bit to more modern times, the main crux of the Law of Attraction teachings come from the late 19th century and the advent of the New Thought movement. This is certainly *not* to be confused with the new age movement, which arose in the 1970s. The New Thought movement was founded upon the philosophies of a group of spiritual thinkers who came together from many different religious backgrounds over common belief. The key players were Emma Curtis Hopkins, Charles and Myrtle Fillmore, Nona L. Brooks, Ernest Holmes, Mary Baker Eddy, Judge Thomas Troward, Wallace Wattles, Napoleon Hill, Emmet Fox, Catherine Ponder, and even Ralph Waldo Emerson and Henry David Thoreau. The first known proponent of New Thought was Phineas Parkhurst Quimby (1801–1866), an American healer, inventor, and mesmerist who believed that illness originated in the mind due to false beliefs and that correcting the mind with God's wisdom would therefore correct the illness. Quimby came upon these beliefs after himself witnessing the power of the mind to heal through hypnosis, placebos, and the power of suggestion. This became a strong tenet of Christian Science, which along with Divine Science, Unity Christianity, and Religious Science made up the teaching systems under the New Thought banner.

The two basic tenets of New Thought are these: The Divine is found in all things, and the mind is more powerful than matter. By changing your thoughts, you change your life. By thinking differently, you create a different outer reality. We create our life experiences through our thoughts—and not just the conscious ones. Each of us is an individualized expression of the One God, the One Mind that is all. By union with the One Mind, we could then use the creative force to change, heal, shape, and mold our outer reality. And that creative force works via thought, especially focused intention.

Another major player, Emma Curtis Hopkins, believed that the Christian Trinity was three aspects of divinity, each playing a different role in history. The three historical epochs she associated with the Trinity were God the Father, God the Son, and God the Mother-Spirit. Her belief was that the new epoch of the Mother aspect of God was coming into fruition along with the changing roles of women in society.

Charles and Myrtle Fillmore co-founded Unity Church, which combined teachings of metaphysics with Christianity, using the Bible and the teachings of Christ as a way to empower followers to find the Divine within.

Keys to the Kingdom

Ernest Holmes, founder of Religious Science, created what is today probably the most widely known of the New Thought systems, the Science of Mind (SOM, which has *nothing* to do with Scientology!). SOM is a system that incorporated metaphysical approaches to mind, thought, and union with the Divine force. Holmes's work stated his firm belief that, through the power of scientific prayer, we could achieve union with the creative force, and thus create what we wanted as part of that force.

Much of the New Thought movement centered on beliefs that support the Law of Attraction, using the mind and thought to achieve success and wealth, healing with the mind, and ultimately finding union with the Divine. Going as far back as 1906 with the publication of William Walker Atkinson's *Thought Vibration or the Law of Attraction in the Thought World*, the self-help book movement is said to be directly tied into New Thought's rise in popularity, although there are publications going back into the 1800s exploring the Law of Attraction, in Warren F. Evans's Mental Cure, *Mental Medicine*, and *Soul and Body*.

This movement is not new by any means.

Scientific Prayer and Mind Treatment

All of these systems utilize "scientific" prayer, or affirmative prayer, as it is also known, as the mechanism by which one could manifest what he/she wants in life. That might be money, or a new car, or healing of cancer, or even just inner peace. The most widely used system of scientific prayer uses a structure made of five steps that make up a "spiritual mind treatment," because the mind is literally being treated to think in a different way. Some systems of New Thought use four steps. All are designed to do the same thing, and they all are a part of the concept behind the Trinity Secret—a code of creation.

Step One: Recognition—This step is the recognition of one presence, one power, one substance, one intelligence, one perfect, whole, complete, and harmonious source. This source is unlimited and infinite. This step basically recognizes God, however the person praying perceives God to be.

The Trinity Secret

Step Two: Identification—This step is where the person praying restates the recognition of the one source, of which he/she is a part with no separation or barriers. This step identifies the person praying as individual expression of the one source, one power, one mind embodying the very nature of the source itself. This allows the person praying to state his or her own personal divinity.

Step Three: Declaration—This step declares that what the person praying speaks is the word of truth and that nothing in his/her mind can deny this truth. The person then declares the condition he/she is praying for, and that he/she fully affirms the achievement of this condition. There is no doubt, no fear, no double-mindedness. This is the Word, the Logos of creation, being sent out into the invisible source to be made manifest.

Step Four: Thanksgiving—This step is where gratitude seals the deal. The person praying declares that he/she is grateful for the condition prayed for being already fulfilled. In other words, you give thanks for the outcome before you see it manifest in the physical world.

Step Five: Release—This is the step where we let it go, and let God, or Source, take over. From this point on, if doubt and fear arise, we do the prayer sequence over again until we fully "feel" the fulfillment of the desired condition. We see the new car in the driveway, feel the happiness of paying off debt, hear the laughter of children we hope to have. We envision it as already a done deal, and we let it go.

All prayers end with a brief completion statement such as "And so it is." This present-tense declaration finishes the treatment and allows the person praying to let it all go and move on, to take the necessary actions he/she is guided to take over the coming days, weeks, months.

"And so it is" is a modernized form of "Amen." Billions of people pray every day, and end their prayers with a word few probably understand. The word itself has its roots in Hebrew, Greek, and Arabic, and is a declaration of affirmation that means "confirmed," "to be firm," and "so be it." The Islamic version also means "so be it." The power of the declaration closes the prayer by sending the word out into the source, to God, to the Universe, to be fulfilled in physical reality. But the reason why most people's prayers don't come to pass is that once the word

Keys to the Kingdom

amen is spoken, any fear or doubt or resistance to that which has been prayed for shuts down the process! More modern uses of "amen" have come to mean something akin to "Isn't it the truth!" or "That's telling it like it is":

- ❧ "Amen, sister!"
- ❧ "Amen to that, brother!"
- ❧ "Can I get an amen, please?"

Saying "amen" or "And so it is" solidifies the supplication and is a declaration of *faith that it will be fulfilled*.

Christ himself warned of being of a double mind. You cannot pray or ask for something, then turn around and have no faith in its fulfillment. It's like putting an order into the Universal Warehouse for something you desire, then immediately calling and canceling that order! The Universe does just what you ask for: It takes what you want, puts it back on the warehouse shelf, and closes the doors.

One of the reasons why prayer and affirmation are often spoken out loud is because of our intuitive understanding of the power of sound. From the Big Bang to the Judeo-Christian "Word" or "Logos" to the Aboriginal tradition of singing objects into existence to the more modern concepts of resonance and vibration as attractive and repulsive, sound is the primal creative force, present even before anything visible was formed. But prayers spoken in the mind also have power, because thought has power. Thought has energy. And as the Trinity Secret tells us, for anything to be created, there needs to be a creative force or middle man between the initial idea and the final result, and thought has creative force. It is one of many "activating agents" that make "something" out of "nothing."

Thought, especially intention, is the middle man between creator and created. It is the reason why some prayers work, and others don't. Why some affirmations take seed, and others don't. Why the Law of attraction works for some, and not for others.

Scientific, or affirmative prayer, does not beg or wish or hope. It is a firm declaration of union with the Divine Force, our role in it, and what we expect to occur in the outer, manifest word. There is no begging or supplication involved. And one of the key words here is *expect*, for no matter how much we pray, it won't come to pass if we don't expect it to. We have to *intend* it to happen. Then we have to *expect* that it already has. Act as if.

The Growing Popularity of the Law of Attraction

So how could a concept so simple to understand and practice not work for so many people? The answer lies in the domain of the Holy Spirit, the aspect of the Trinity least understood, but most critical for anything to be created, whether on a cosmic or microcosmic scale.

Today's Law of Attraction movement has become a mega-entity in itself, spawning hundreds of books, movies, television and radio programs, Websites, seminars, and classes all devoted to trying to teach us what the ancients recognized, but perhaps did not fully comprehend, in the triune nature of creation. Authors such as Dr. Wayne Dyer, Deepak Chopra, Sandra Anne Taylor, Esther and Jerry Hicks, and a million others have turned the self-help world on its head with the idea that we attract to us what we think about and believe. This is a billion-dollar industry, evident of the general dissatisfaction of the public and the desire for a better life.

Unfortunately, the entire Law of Attraction movement appears to have fallen prey to the more sensational aspects of people promising incredible wealth in seven days, or a soul mate in a month. This belies a terrible misunderstanding of the forces at work—forces that even our ancestors revered as powerful and effective if harnessed and utilized in the correct way. The hunger for get-rich-quick schemes has created an industry ready to cater to the desire for the easiest way out possible. And wow, to tell someone all he/she had to do was think about something and he/she would get it? It definitely doesn't get any easier than that!

Except it isn't easy. Not by any means. Yet every day people manage to use the threefold process of creation to manifest their outer reality—for better or worse.

The problem begins with a general lack of understanding of the three aspects themselves, and how they work together to produce what we see in the explicate order of things. If you don't understand the way the process itself works, and what drives and directs it, no amount of thought or intention will get you anything more than a headache.

The Father: God, Source, Allness, Superimplicate, Creator. Whatever name this aspect goes by, it is the one who creates. It's that simple. When we think of the word *God*, we think of the driver of the car of creation, the one who decides which direction the car is going to go. It is the intelligence and energetic wellspring from which things are expressed through the explicate order. It makes things, including us human beings.

The Son: Christ, Lord, Light, Man, Manifest, and Divine in Human Form. This is the physical expression of what the creator intended to create. This is the creation itself. This is the manifest, explicate order. Reality. What is right in front of your face. The Universe we live in.

The Holy Spirit: Breath, yeast, activating agent, thought, consciousness, wind, intention, creative force. This is where the creator creates creation. It is the active force needed to produce an actual physical manifestation out of the field of all possibilities. Stuff stays in the field unless there is a way for it to take form, shape, matter, and be made manifest. This is where most people get tripped up when dealing with the secret behind not only the Law of attraction, but the Trinity itself.

Two Levels of Creation

You can have a creator. You can see creation. But can you understand the process of creation? Because without it, nothing ever gets created!

It happens on two levels: the cosmic and the microcosmic. We can start with the big stuff.

How was the Universe and all that it contains made, and who or what made it? Whether you believe in intelligent design or pure scientific order, it is hard to believe that the intricacy by which our universe came to exist was nothing but random luck. Chance. A fluke. In many of our previous books we've discussed the presence of mathematical principles and ratios that underlie the forces of the Universe—ratios that, if tweaked ever so slightly, would have resulted in nothing. No planets, no stars, no chemicals by which life could have ever arisen. Sounds like there might have been a little thought that went into the process!

Even the non-religious can recognize a blueprint when they see it, as if some Master Architect had drawn out the structure of what would become our Universe, including the emergence of life. And because it all seems to be based upon numbers, we might say that there was a Master Mathematician at the helm of the ship. Before we are labeled heretics and disbelievers, this in no way implies that the creator is in any way human, or even close to being human. Instead, it implies that the creator has the ability, somehow, to think. To intend. To have consciousness. Like the Mind of God Hermes wrote of. And that everything we see in our Universe is the physical manifestation of a thought in the mind of God.

Let's go with that for a bit.

This creator is a neutral force. It knows nothing of good or bad. It is pretty much all encompassing but does not judge. In other words, it is indifferent and impartial. And not necessarily in a bad way.

The creator made creation. We see that. We know that there is a physical order. We live in it.

But what are the means by which a cosmic creator creates creation?

Natural laws and fundamental forces that serve to create matter are all a part of the directive. Behind it all there must first be some kind of intention to put these laws and forces to work in the first place. So the Mind of God seeks to express itself and does so by producing the infinite and endless Universe and filling it with all kinds of places, people, and things. It thinks, and it manifests. The Big Bang, and whatever happened before it, were active intentions to create a universe where before there was only the void. Nothingness. If that were not the case, we would not be here. Someone or something had to have decided to (pardon us, Nike) "just do it." And that includes creating not only the diversity of life we see, but how evolution seems to fit right in with a grand design.

Keys to the Kingdom

Two very highly regarded physical theorists, Stephen Hawking and Roger Penrose, have both determined that there is a definite beginning for time in the Universe. This beginning can be established by examining the behavior of light, and means that when our Universe began, so did time. Prior to the Big Bang, then, there may have been no dimensions of time and space, just that nothingness or primordial void from which all things emerged. This void would be eternal in both time and space. But something made something out of this void of nothingness. Some action occurred by which the Big Bang of our universe went Bang!

Many scientists agree. Quoted from the Website *www.godandscience .org*, the following scientists speak about the design of the Universe:

Paul Davies, physicist—"There is for me powerful evidence that there is something going on behind it all.... It seems as though somebody has fine-tuned nature's numbers to make the Universe.... The impression of design is overwhelming."

Arthur Eddington, astrophysicist—"The idea of a universal mind or Logos would be, I think, a fairly plausible inference from the present state of scientific theory."

Bernard Haisch, astrophysicist—"A Creator capable of cleverly designing a few basic laws of physics in such a way as to permit the tremendous complexity of life to evolve is, to me, more impressive than a Creator who has to tinker around with making creatures—with some striking failures along the way."

Fred Hoyle, astrophysicist—"A common sense interpretation of the facts suggests that a superintellect has monkeyed with physics, as well as with chemistry and biology, and that there are no blind forces worth speaking about in nature."

Vera Kistiakowsky, physicist—"The exquisite order displayed by our scientific understanding of the physical world calls for the divine."

The Trinity Secret

Wernher von Braun, pioneer rocketry engineer—"I find it as difficult to understand a scientist who does not acknowledge the presence of a superior rationality behind the existence of the universe as it is to understand a theologian who would deny the advances of science."

Chandra Wickrasinge, scientist: "[Genuine science supports] some miraculous property of life that's either explained in terms of a statistical miracle or in terms of an intelligent intervening. It's one or the other."

Arno Penzias, physicist—"Astronomy leads us to a unique event, a universe which was created out of nothing, one with the very delicate balance needed to provide exactly the conditions to permit life, and one which has an underlying (o ne might say 'supernatural') plan."

The problems arise when religious belief enters the fray. "God" becomes either a Hebrew God or a Christian God or a God that fits into any number of traditions we hold near and dear. But the creator may be nothing more than consciousness, a universal consciousness that has an awareness we do not understand. We barely understand our own consciousness. Imagine, though, that there is *some* type of creator that made all this. Name it; frame it any way you want. Just imagine.

The whole of creation is that which has been, and continuously is created. That's the easiest part of all, because it is where we live, who we are. It is us.

Laws of Creation

So we can imagine the Father/Creator, and we know the Son/ Creation. Where we get tripped up is the act of creation itself.

In cosmic terms, scientists look to known physical laws by which our universe is structured, formed, and sustained. We understand that there are four fundamental forces at work: gravity, electromagnetism, and the weak and strong nuclear forces. We know that there are a number of mathematical ratios that describe the creation of stars and planets and the chemical processes necessary for life. And we know that nature has its patterns and cycles that allow for the evolution, adaptation, and sometimes extinction of species. These laws and patterns and ratios are the active agents behind creation. But there may be another element involved.

Ervin Laszlo, in *Beliefs About Evolution, Mind, Nature and Society*, ponders a collective consciousness that may make up a self-aware universe. This great Mind or Cosmic Entity might be subject to the same laws observed in our physical universe, such as the Law of Energy Conservation, but Laszlo proposes there might also be a "psi field," or psychic field. This field, comparable to a gravitational and electromagnetic field, would be where all individual experience is accumulated and deposited at the cosmic level. This field, he stresses, would possess a "mental dimension" and therefore be the mental dimension of our Universe—a cosmic "Mind."

Some folks who espouse a more mystical or philosophical bent suggest that thought, intention, and consciousness are also activating agents in the process and direction of creation. Some in the scientific community are also suggesting this might actually be the case, especially in the quantum world where conscious observation plays a distinct role in the behavior of particles and waves. Consciousness may be the link between the cosmic All and the individual human being. The Creator might actually think, albeit not like we do. The thoughts of the Creator may manifest physicality, albeit not like we can. The consciousness of the Creator may unfold and evolve and know itself by even greater expression of diversity of life, albeit not in a way we fully understand. Yet sages tell us "As Above, So Below."

The Practical Use of the Trinity Secret

Whatever the creative process behind the cosmos truly is, it works because we are here as proof. The question becomes: Does the same process work in us?

This is where the Trinity Secret hits close to home. For what is a secret if it cannot be used in a practical, human sense?

What works on the cosmic level also works in us. But there is a reversal of roles. In the cosmic code, we act as the Son, the physical manifestation of the Father through the creative process of the Holy Spirit. Or, to put it outside of Trinitarian terms, we are the explicate result of the superimplicate working in the enfolding and unfolding of the implicate.

But on the individual level, the microcosmic, we are now given the role of creator, the Father. Each person is a creator, or perhaps as we shall see, a co-creator, of his/her reality. Obviously, there are elements of our existence that were put into place as a part of the cosmic creative process: We do not make trees, or the oceans, or the sun. The cosmic creator is responsible for much of what we see and perceive collectively (and this is where many law of attraction detractors find fault with the whole "Secret" secret…).

The statement "You create your own reality" does not mean that you create the entirety of the universe. It means that you create your own reality *within the confines of your time and space in that universe*. No amount of thought, intention, or conscious awareness is going to change the sun or stop the moon from rising. You can't change the wind, or stop a rock from being a rock, but you can create and control the outcome of much of what occurs in your own individual corner of the space/time continuum.

We are each a universe within ourselves. And this is the domain of the microcosmic Trinity, where we are the Creator, and the day-to-day life we live is what we have created, consciously or not. One of the basic tenets of the Law of Attraction requires you to look at your life as a mirror of the sum total of your past choices, thoughts, actions, desires, and intentions. The explicate order of our lives is the "living proof" that this code of creation works in us just as it does on a cosmic scale. The things that we want tend to manifest, even if we don't really want them. Have you ever heard the saying "You can never get enough of what you don't want"? Blame the Law of Attraction for this. We may think we want something, but once we actually make it happen, we realize it was the worst possible thing for us. Think of someone who wants to win the lottery, only to find that when he/she does so that life becomes far more

Keys to the Kingdom

complicated, with people wanting money and help and assistance. Be careful for what you wish for, because the Law of Attraction will give it to you!

Or rather, blame the middle man. The most difficult aspect of the Trinity, the Holy Spirit, is also representative of the one part of the Law of Attraction that most people just can't seem to master. We can act like creators. We can see what we've created. But we cannot for the life of us figure out how we did it, or how to change it. That is what occurs in the domain of the implicate, the hidden, unseen order where forces animate and activate our thoughts, intentions, and consciousness, and mold them into something tangible we can experience on a sensory level. In *The Evolutionary Mind: Conversations on Science, Imagination and Spirit*, Rupert Sheldrake discusses the mystical Trinity, describing the Holy Spirit element as "the moving principle," always conceived in the Bible as some type of moving image (wind, fire, flame, a bird in flight): "The idea is that the spirit is inherently unpredictable, a moving principle, present in all people, all of nature and containing the element of surprise. There's also the formative principle, the Logos, which gives things their form. The Logos evolves as creation evolves, and there's always this dynamical Spirit within it."

In *Sun of God: Discover the Self-Organizing Consciousness That Underlies Everything*, author Gregory Sams equates the Holy Spirit to the Christian equivalent of a universal field of spirit, a field of energy that all cultures seem to have understood in their own way. To the Great Sioux Nation, this was the Wakan-Tanka, the Great Mystery and source of all power, and to the ancient Greeks, it was Mind, infused in all of nature, giving it intelligence and form. Sams points out how modern Christian Church doctrine has such difficulty with the Holy Spirit element of the Trinity, finding it hard to explain and hard to describe, yet crying heresy for those who do (we are sure we will be among them!). According to Sams, "Whatever it is named, the divine spirit is always perceived to be something with which our consciousness is fundamentally intertwined, whether we act in that knowledge or not." This universal consciousness, then, that pervades all matter in existence, and is the stuff from which all unmanifest matter will arise, is "the vibrational DNA of the universe."

The Trinity Secret

This is critical to understand. Sheldrake goes on to say, "The Holy Trinity has process within it, the Spirit being the breath, the Word being the spoken word." The historical perspective has always made the Trinity into some type of obscure object, a description of the Divine. But as Sheldrake states, and as we propose, *it is a process!* An ancient process understood by those who came before us.

The active spirit, the element of movement, is where the works of the Father are manifested in the world of the Son. And the use of sound, the Word, is instrumental in bringing things into form. Sheldrake describes it as "the vibratory coming forth of things in time," and that this is the very essence of divine nature. He refers to the work of Matthew Fox, who described the "Cosmic Christ" as the "cosmic, creative process with consciousness, meaning and a vibratory nature." The entirety of the Universe is this Cosmic Christ. "It is a divine, creative cosmos."

This concept of a creative cosmos, one that is continually evolving and progressing, is a part of Process Theology, originating with the works of Alfred North Whitehead. Process Theology looks at "God" as being relational to humans, not unilaterally controlling humans. God has a "will" in everything, but not everything that occurs is God's will. The divine power becomes, then, relational and not controlling, allowing for progressive growth and a continuous dynamic evolution. God is changeable, but there is also a part of God that is fixed, eternal, unchangeable. So there is a part of God, and all of creation, that is ever-changing, moving toward constant growth and evolution, never complete or finished.

An evolving God, a progressive Cosmic Consciousness, a divine process. That same process is happening down here, below, in the human realm. If God the Father is fixed, and God the Son is expressed, then God the Holy Spirit is the process. All are One, yet all are individual. All are part of the whole, yet all can be separated into elements of the One. It always comes back to the same thing. Not a "persona," but a process.

This malleable element of creativity, if you will, is where the power of the spirit resides. This is where the creative force does its work. This is where we find the fixed truths and the changing realities. And this is where the Law of Attraction does its thing.

Keys to the Kingdom

Why doesn't the law work for so many people? Simple. Because they don't work the law.

The Five Steps of Prayer and the Trinity

Going back to scientific prayer for a minute, the five steps lay out the Trinity Secret itself, making it a much more effective form of prayer than the usual "Dear God, please help me, save me…" that most of us engage in. The first two steps, Recognition and Unification, identify the Father, the Creator, and how we are united with that source as co-creators. The last two steps, Thanksgiving and Release, are the Son, the manifest, where we already recognize it as being a done deal. The middle step—and it's always the middle one that gets us—is Realization, or as some say, Declaration. This is where we lay down the order we want the Universe to fulfill. The more detail, the better, and the more feeling and certainty behind it, the better. This is the domain of the Holy Spirit.

In his book *Secrets of the Lost Mode of Prayer: The Hidden Power of Beauty, Blessing, Wisdom and Hurt,* author and visionary Gregg Braden states, "Whether it was conscious or not, the ancients apparently understood how to address the field of energy that connects everything." When it comes to the use of prayer for healing, Braden believes that if we learn to "speak to that field" in a manner that the field understands, we can literally change the "genetic blueprint." He suggests a three-part structured prayer that is analogous to a computer program:

1. Initialization Statements—These create the initial opening or feeling of unification. They give us the tools we need for the program to work.
2. Work Statements—Here we do our calculations to get something done. We set intentions. We ask for something specific in prayer.
3. Closure or Completion Statements—This brings it all to a complete end, and declares that it is all done. Closure. Amen.

These are the same concepts that make up scientific prayer, and again stress that first one must identify with the creator or creative source, then tell it what you want, then declare it is already done.

The Trinity Secret

The usual prayer bypasses these most important steps of identifying our role in the process of creation. Most Christian prayers begin with "In the name of the Father, the Son, and the Holy Spirit," or end with that same statement, followed by "Amen," the final word that proves our faith and sets it all in stone. But it's what is put into the body of the prayer that often neutralizes the outcome. Begging does not work. Down here on the human level, the source, the Cosmic Mind, the great consciousness or force, or whatever, is neutral—and even more importantly, it will give you what you want and desire. It will give you what you speak and think about. It will give you what your subconscious tells it to. So, if you beg, "God, please help save me from this pain," the Cosmic Mind hears only that you are experiencing pain, and gives you more pain to experience. Why? Not because it is mean, but because you have *affirmed the pain.*

Do not affirm what you do not want!

The words of a prayer are meaningless unless they are spoken with conviction, belief, and focused intention, almost like a demand. Otherwise, they are powerless to the deeper held beliefs and convictions of the subconscious. The Law of Attraction teachings tells us that we get exactly what our dominant thoughts ask for. If we spend most of our time complaining about our situation, talking about it, thinking about it, hating how much our lives suck, that is exactly what we will get more of, simply because that is what is dominating our thoughts and our actions. Going to bed at night and praying for release then becomes only a drop in the bucket already filled with poisoned water.

Imagine a block of clay. You take the clay and mold it however you want. You can make a ball, or a dog, or a sailboat. The clay itself doesn't judge or care. It becomes what you want it to become. For so many people who purchased *The Secret* or watched the film, the basic lack of understanding of the neutrality of universal energy is what kept them from making any change. Dr. Wayne Dyer, a pioneer in the self-help and personal empowerment fields, has a great saying that should be taken to heart: "What you focus on, expands." Source doesn't give a damn what you want; it will give it to you.

If your focus is on how much you lack, then you attract more lack. That is the order you've place to the Universal Warehouse, and that is the order that will be delivered to your door. It doesn't matter how many affirmations you do in between—if your dominant thoughts are of *lack*, you will get a lot more of it. For most people, our dominant thoughts arise from our subconscious beliefs, not from our conscious beliefs. You may say you believe in love, but if your subconscious harbors fears of rejection and heartache from past experiences, you really do not believe in love. You want it on a conscious level. You may desire to make more money, but if something in your subconscious is telling you that you are not worthy, you will continue to only make what you believe you are worth. First you have to clean out the cobwebs in the subconscious and reprogram it with the thoughts and intentions and beliefs of what you really and truly do want.

Double-mindedness and half-heartedness mold the clay of source energy into something that is only half-assed. The spirit element of the Trinity animates and activates what we ask it to. If our intention is not firm, and our faith is not solid, we can expect a half-assed response. In a sense, you get what you pay for (or pray for!).

Biology of Belief

We are always using the Law of Attraction. We are always aware of the Trinity within. The problem is that we aren't aware that it is constantly listening to our thoughts, watching our actions, and reacting to the dominant desires we have. Always. As Bruce Lipton states in *The Biology of Belief*, your subconscious programming takes over the second your conscious mind stops paying attention, and with all the distractions of modern life, that happens a lot! The subconscious always operates in the present moment, paying attention to everything we think, say, and do, even when we are not.

But, even when we are paying attention, and doing our affirmations and thinking happy positive thoughts, like we are told, the subconscious programming of old is still running the show. It is up to the conscious mind—our free will—Lipton says, to "step in, stop the behavior, and create a new response."

Lipton sums it up with this: "The biggest impediments to realizing the successes of which we dream are the limitations programmed into the subconscious." Our behavior, even our health and physiology, is influenced by this programming. We are, indeed, the result of what we are programmed to believe. Some studies show that when a conscious belief comes into conflict with a pre-existing belief stored in the subconscious, the conflict can be expressed by a weakening of the body's muscles. Most of us have heard of the popular kinesiology experiment of muscle testing by putting both arms out in front of the body, then asking two questions, one true, and one false, while someone pushes down on the arms. Surprisingly, or maybe not so surprisingly, the arms will resist with great strength when a truth is stated, but the mistruth or lie will cause the arm muscles to go weak and easily be pushed down. The subconscious, you see, tells and knows the truth.

Marie's Secret Story

I got *The Secret* when it came out, but already had a long history with religious science teachings and metaphysics. I knew all about the Law of Attraction, but rarely took the time or energy to consciously put it to work in my life.

Around this time, I had gotten divorced and wanted to sell my house. This was during the height of the real estate bust in the area I lived, and every house for sale in my area was either in foreclosure, or selling for way less than what the owners had paid for it. I made it my goal to sell my house for at least a $100,000 profit. I never let up on that goal. Using the Law of Attraction teachings, I focused on what I wanted—the outcome I desired—not ever giving in to the fears of my realtor, who told me I was crazy, or my neighbors, who told me I was out of my mind.

I "acted" as if what I wanted was already a done deal and began to think about how I would save the money, what I would pay off first, all the things I could do with it. I never let up, knowing that as soon as enough doubt and fear trickled in, the goal would be sabotaged. It was one of the hardest things I've ever done, keeping my faith, belief, and intention on track 24/7, but I needed to prove to myself this worked, because if it worked on a house, it would work on other, more important things.

Sure enough, after about four months, my house sold for the highest price of any in the area (despite being the smallest model!) and I came out of it with $104,500 profit. Luck? Nope. I wanted it. I believed it. I made it happen.

Since then, I've often forgotten to watch my focus, and have paid the price for it, but I have managed to attract a lot of good things into my life when I do. Researching this book convinces me even more that I am a creative person in more ways than one!

Once, though, we are able to see the same creative threefold process that is at work in the cosmos at work in ourselves, we begin to realize the importance of taking responsibility for our roles as creators. This is the first step to better understanding how to use the wind and breath and fire of the universal energy, the Holy Spirit moving through us, to create a reality that we can not only live with, but love.

The Teachings of Neville Goddard

The next time you order something from the Universe, make sure it is what you want on every level, because if that is your dominant thought, you will get it. It's what you intend that manifests. Put a little emotion and passion behind that focused intention, to really make it happen. This is a concept known as "Nevillizing," based upon the teachings of Neville Goddard, an amazing metaphysical thinker and writer. Coined by Law of Attraction author and speaker Joe Vitale, the act of Nevillizing means to basically "act as if"—as if you already possess the thing or quality you seek. This goes far beyond just affirming something, or thinking positively. This means you continuously pretend you have already fulfilled the desire you intended to fulfill!

Goddard, born in 1905 in Barbados, taught throughout the United States, lecturing and writing about "the law," which we might equate with "The Secret." The Law was that you simply used imagination to change physical reality. The power of the mind was amazing, and by imagining, you could actually become what you imagined. He encouraged people to use their "imaginal power," or power of the imagination, not just for their own personal gain, but for the benefit of humanity as well.

Just imagining something doesn't work unless the intention behind it is strong, focused, and exact. As Goddard taught, constant and persistent imagining is what worked, and one had to truly take on the feelings, emotions, and actions of a person who has already fulfilled the desire he/she wished. He also talked about the importance of seeing the end result in one's mind. For example, if you wanted to get a promotion, you acted as if you already had that promotion—dressing the part, speaking the part, even imagining over and over shaking hands with your boss as he/she tells you about your new office and higher salary. It is all about *feeling* your way into a new reality, not just thinking.

The Power of Intention

What is intention? Focused, directed, persistent thought. It is resolve and determination to make a specific thing happen. It is repeated thought and action toward a particular goal. Intention, both individual and collective, can change reality. Intention is how we change reality. Carlos Castaneda described intention in his book *The Active Side of Infinity* as "a force that exists in the universe. When sorcerers (those who live off the Source) beckon intent, it comes to them and sets up the path for attainment, which means that sorcerers always accomplish what they set out to do."

Intention happens both on the individual and the universal scale. There is an intention behind every creation in the Universe. In *The Power of Intention*, Dr. Wayne Dyer looks at the hidden field of intention as a force we all have access to, and can make use of and tap into. This force even directs every aspect of nature, turning a tiny acorn into a mighty oak tree. "Nature simply progresses in harmony from the field of intention. We, too, are intended from the energy of this field."

Dyer states that we all have the ability to use this field of intention; however, most of us choose not to even recognize it. Our erred belief that we are separate from Source disallows us to access this field. "Activating intention means rejoining your Source and becoming a modern day sorcerer. Being a sorcerer means attaining the level of awareness where previously inconceivable things are available." What the minds of men can conceive, men can achieve, to paraphrase a famous saying.

But if that intention is not also grounded in the subconscious, it will not come to pass. The subjective mind, the realm of the subconscious, is more in tune with the collective mind of the Universe than our conscious mind. In the subjective every thought is accepted, good or bad, and the dominant thoughts placed into it become our belief and perception of the world around us. Our belief and perception become our reality.

Think of the conscious mind as the one that chooses or decides. It initiates things—gets the ball rolling. The subjective or subconscious mind is the active, productive mind, taking whatever is handed to it by the conscious mind, and making it happen, man! Thus, what we consciously think is what we subconsciously create: "I am so fat." "I hate being poor." "He doesn't love me." "All women are gold diggers." "These books are so hard to write." The bad gets thrown in with the good and either cancels out anything from manifesting, or, depending on the balance of powers, the winner takes all. Garbage in, garbage out.

The only way to override the contents of the subconscious or subjective mind is by controlling what we put into it from our conscious mind. Intention is a tool not only for creating but also for changing what we create. It requires a strong commitment and will, a determination to keep the focus on what is actually desired, all the while deflecting thoughts about what is no longer desired. But only when we realize we are a part of the field of intention in the first place, can we really access that tool and make use of it. This is the part of scientific prayer where we identify ourselves as one with Source. We recognize. We represent!

For this very reason, many intention teachers suggest meditation or some form of calming the left brain, analytical mind, as a means for getting in the right "state of mind" to create powerful intention. Anything that alters consciousness to a relaxed, focused state will work, whether it be running, praying, or even listening to uplifting music. But try to set an intention while distracted and distressed and it just won't take hold. Getting the mind in the proper receptive mode is the first step. Keeping the focus on the specific thought of what is wanted is the second. And probably the most important of all is the third step: knowing that it is already on its way, and being grateful and expectant of it. This is how you pray. This is how you create. This is how you manifest.

There is one more step, and one that most people don't ever take, involved in the creation of anything: action. You cannot pray for something without also taking action toward receiving it. Action that is directed by intuition, inner guidance and synchronicities that are put on our path to keep us moving in the right direction, toward the goal, not away from it. Without action, no amount of praying, intending, or demanding will move the forces of the Universe. Remember the old joke about the man who prayed every night to win the lottery? Over and over he prayed, but nothing happened. Finally he got pissed and pleaded with God, "I prayed every night to win the lottery. Why have you forsaken me? Please, God, let me win the lottery!" And God sighed with frustration and said, "Well, I would if you would go out and buy a damn ticket!"

There are a number of great books out there on the Law of Attraction and intention (many of which are listed in the Bibliography). But reading a book and trying a few things won't cut it. As Yoda once said, "Do or do not. There is no try." Intention does not respond to *try*. Try, and it will give you exactly what you asked for: more trying. *Try* is a positive-sounding word with a negative intention. "I will try" means that there is a chance you will not, and that is what the field of intention hears. The "will" is canceled out by the "will not," both being potentialities. That old double-mindedness trips you up every time.

One of the most fascinating books out there is from the author of *The Field*, Lynne McTaggart. In *The Intention Experiment*, she delves into the subject of personal and collective intention, and has even set up a Website (*www.theintentionexperiment.com*) where she conducts collective intention experiments in order to determine if there is indeed a formative, creative power to the focused thoughts of many minds working together for a singular goal. There are weekly intentions one can take part in, and larger experiments that could one day prove that a collective consciousness truly does exist and is at work in our reality.

Keys to the Kingdom

This collective intention adds another level of responsibility to our role as creators, for if we indeed can help shape the world itself with our intention, it behooves us to make those intentions as positive as possible. Why intend war, hatred, and poverty when we have the very same ability to intend their opposites? Maybe our existence here on earth is nothing but one giant intention experiment, again begging the question: Who or what intended us into being? Or, did we somehow intend ourselves into being?

We the authors also encourage readers to follow the work of IONS, the Institute of Noetic Sciences (*www.noetic.org*), founded by former Apollo astronaut Edgar Mitchell, who experienced a profound sense of Samadhi, or universal connectedness, on the way back to earth from a trip to the moon. He wrote about the experience and how it changed his entire world view in his book, *The Way of the Explorer.* This experience changed Mitchell, and opened him up to a new worldview and a new understanding of his own place within that worldview. The word *noetic* comes from the Greek word *nous*, which means "intuitive mind" or "inner knowing." The institute is devoted to the study of human consciousness and how and why it matters. The goal of IONS is advancing the science of consciousness and human experience to serve individual and collective transformation. Noetics is indeed the science of the future of humanity.

Strangely enough, it took a popular best-selling book by Dan Brown called *The Lost Symbol* to put both the work of Lynn McTaggart and IONS into the public's view. In his book, Brown discussed intention, the field, and human consciousness, and he exposed these higher ideas to millions of readers, who hungrily then devoured the works Brown mentioned, boosting sales of McTaggart's books, among others. We focus so much on the outer world, the cosmos, the final frontier of space and time. But Noetics is drawing us to the final frontier of the inner universe—the human mind, consciousness, spirit. We are the cosmos, turned inward.

Criticisms of the Law of Attraction Teachings

We live in two worlds, straddling them as if sitting upon a fence, legs dangling on either side. We live in the world of cosmic creation, where the source or All acts as the shaper and molder of the hidden energies, creating our ever-evolving world. We also live in the world of human creation, where we step into the position of the creator, and shape and mold the hidden energies to create our own ever-evolving place in the sun. Often we forget that we do create on a daily basis, and this lack of awareness and insight may explain the ease by which so many people harm or abuse themselves, and others. Not to mention why so many people lead lives of regret, unhappiness, and lack of fulfillment. When you believe you are not in the driver's seat, you allow yourself to be driven anywhere—even places you never wanted to go.

Critics of the Law of Attraction have attacked the teachings on the basis that if we attract and think our reality into being, why would there be war, violence, death, and disease? Why would children die and be abused? Why would some be born into privilege and others into horrible poverty? First of all, many of these horrors are human-originated. And we must face the fact that we are all interconnected, even if we cannot see it because it occurs on the implicate order. Our web of connectivity allows us to make choices, decisions, and actions that affect those around us. It is, to some degree, our fault that these things exist. These are the things we can change, but often do not choose to.

Understanding that the process of the Trinity Secret happens on two levels can explain some of the parts of life we consider or judge to be wrong. We as humans have no control over the cosmic creators' works. This cosmic creative force knows no good or evil. It is All. And that includes some things we judge as bad. Disasters happen. Weather does not obey the desires of man. Diseases strike. Nature cycles through creation, destruction, and re-creation. Someone is born blind, someone is born with deformities, and someone is born with a terminal illness that takes his/her life away at a painfully early age. The rules and the laws are those of the creative force that put us all here, and until we discover our own individual link to cosmic mind, and enough of us do so, we cannot change cosmic mind. In fact, we cannot even understand the true meaning of these events, if indeed there is a meaning. For some, it's karma, debt from a past life, or a role in a lesson to be learned. Maybe so. But we all know there are things that happen that we cannot change. (That is why we have the Serenity Prayer!)

On our level of creation, we do have power, and we can change and control much of what becomes our reality. War, many diseases, poverty, abuse, and violence are all within the control of each individual and the collective of humanity. Knowing the truth that we are, on a deeper level, all one organism, one mind, one soul, we would stop treating those around us in horrific and brutal ways. Because ultimately, we would also be hurting ourselves. The web of life includes everyone and everything. We are all connected on that hidden implicate order.

Were we to all work the Trinity Secret for the eradication and elimination of these things, we would see them come to an end. Until then, we must take the lives we were given and create what we want, change what we can, and accept what we cannot change. The cosmic creator is growing, evolving, and encouraging us to use our choice, free will, and intention to do the same. It won't force us; that is not the kind of "God" it is.

Knowing we indeed have the power to change, to create, to transform is a responsibility few are willing to take on.

It requires, first, the courage to know we can.

That which IS is manifested;
That which has been or shall be, is unmanifested, but not dead;
For soul, the eternal activity of God, animates all things.
—Hermes

Conclusion:
Many Mansions,
Many Roads

I bind myself today; The strong name of the Trinity, By invocation of the same; The Three in One and One in Three
—Cecil Frances Alexander

We dance 'round in a ring and suppose, while the secret sits in the middle and knows.
—Robert Frost

No man can reveal to you nothing but that which already lies half-asleep in the dawning of your knowledge.
—Kahlil Gibran

Imagine hundreds of thousands of years ago, a group of primitive men and women sitting around a roaring fire, looking up at the stars in awe. Talking. Wondering. Asking questions. Seeking answers. Imagine thousands of years ago: sages writing in secret about their ideas that, if made known, might label them heretics. Secrets about how things above happen below. How the heavens are mirrored in the souls of men. How the world seems to work in a triune fashion. Asking questions. Seeking answers. Now, imagine today:

students in colleges all over the world meeting for discussion groups, pondering the scientific achievements and advances of the 21st century, and wondering where our place is in all of it. Are we creating this? What is reality? Can we change our lives? Asking questions. Seeking answers.

Since the dawn of humanity, the goal of understanding who we are, how we got here, and why, has driven mankind's unquenchable thirst for knowledge. The questions have always been the same. It's the answers that seem to keep changing. As a society, as we become more and more scientifically advanced and technologically adept, we continue to unlock the door to some of the mysteries of the cosmos, our bodies, and the natural world around us. But we still don't know very much. What or who started it all? How did it all get "created"? Is what we see really real, or is it simply an illusion created by our perception? Can we alter or change this subjective reality merely by imagining and intending a different vision? Is the mind that powerful? Can belief or intention really heal, kill, or move mountains? Why are we here? What is the purpose of it all?

Maybe we aren't meant to get all the answers until we first "get" the basic lesson of the creative process—how we got here, and how we ourselves get things here. Perhaps we first need to recognize our own role in the bigger picture before we can set about changing that bigger picture. Maybe we are only intended to uncover our power a little at a time, so we can hopefully learn to treat it with the respect, reverence, and responsibility required.

Then again, what if we've had the answers right in front of us all along, but thought them too simple—too obvious—to be true? Hidden in plain sight, the last place we would ever think to look. Obvious, yet occult and shaded, veiled from the intellect but recognizable to the heart, the spirit, and the soul. Knowledge that is intuited rather than rationalized.

Occam's Razor tells us that the simplest of explanations is often the best. The Trinity Secret is that simplest of explanations of how creation came to exist, minus the details and minutiae that really have no cogent bearing upon our normal, average human lives. This simple secret not only tells us just how powerful and responsible we truly are, but throws open the doors to communication and understanding based upon common grounds. In the power of the 3 we find not only the archetype of creation, but our link to the divine—a link in which it might be argued that perhaps we have always known, but somehow have forgotten. Deep down inside of each of us is the realization that we are so much more than just flesh and blood—that we have power and ability to take an idea and with action make it into something real and tangible. This power comes with a huge responsibility to use it for the good of the one and of the many, yet unfortunately, we see evidence of this power being horribly misused every single day in the news headlines.

If everyone on this planet truly understood this secret, how different might be the world in which we live? If we spent just a minute—just 60 short seconds—every day contemplating the threefold order of the Universe, and of our own reality, could we possibly change ourselves enough to influence our surroundings, thus changing others? Or do we continue to walk around in a zombie-like state, not taking any responsibility for our thoughts, choices, or actions, blaming everything and anything for our miserable lives all the while refusing to look inside where the secret sits in the center and knows?

The secret has been sitting there all along. It's been right under our noses since time immemorial. Perhaps all it required of us was a slight change of perception.

Not only do all of the major and minor religious systems share in this powerful Trinity symbolism, but so, too, do our psychological and cultural systems. By examining the Trinity as a means of understanding the spiritual nature of man, the psychological nature of the mind, and the "pseudo-physical" nature of God, we find many parallels of thought and belief that can serve to form the basis for more tolerance and understanding between diverse cultures.

If the basic metaphysical concept of the Holy Trinity as a process by which creation is created is understood in some form or another throughout the world, then therefore it is perfectly reasonable to conclude that we are all seekers seeking the same thing. Having such a powerful quest in common should in fact unite us all the more, even if the semantics we use to describe that quest are different.

Many Mansions, Many Roads

In a social context, to know that a Christian can use prayer to reach a state of oneness with God just as a Buddhist across the globe can meditate to achieve a state of Nirvana, or Nothingness, is to know that we all share common goals and desires. We can celebrate the diversity of the ways in which we seek to achieve those goals, while always recognizing that in the end the goal is always the same. None of us is immune to our roles as creators, no matter how much we wish to pass on the responsibility to someone else.

Affirming the Power of the Trinity

Trinities are everywhere, if we but look for them. St. Bonaventure wrote in *The Threefold Way* that he, much like Augustine before him, had seen "trinities everywhere in creation." Bonaventure genuinely believed that the Trinity could "be proved by unaided natural reason" while avoiding the dangers of rationalism by emphasizing the importance of "spiritual experience as an essential component of the idea of God." Thus, anyone could be the Son, using the spiritual experience of the Holy Spirit, to access God the Father. Upon doing so, the Son obtains the same creative power and role as the Father, and the ability, then, to mold creation to his will and intent. Such a simple concept would, indeed, show up just about everywhere one looks in the realm of spirituality and religious experience!

When examined within a personal context, the understanding of the metaphysical basis of the Trinity serves as a simple, yet profound, answer to a riddle asked throughout the ages: Can man and God be one and the same? And if so, how? By utilizing affirmative prayer, meditation, chanting, devotion, service, and any other means that produce a transcendent state of consciousness, we can each experience the Christ within, or the Buddha or Krishna within. We can each experience the essence of Spirit moving in and through us, the Spirit in which we live and move and have our being. This force is not relegated only to the Jedi few (as the *Star Wars* films might suggest!), but to anyone who "hath understanding" of the key to the kingdom of heaven; that the key itself is within, and that it is always accessible. This is the "living water"

Jesus spoke of in John 4:10—the water that takes away all thirst, the water that becomes "a perpetual spring within."

Whether it be living water, or the Logos, or yeast of fire, the truth of the Holy Spirit uniting God and man and activating the creative forces comes in many descriptive forms, but those forms matter not, for they have as their foundation the same idea. Wiccan Priestess and author Laurie Cabot sums it up wonderfully when she says in *The Power of the Witch*:

> This is the basis for all religion—to let the light in, to let Divine Wisdom in. Mystics in every religious tradition speak of alpha states of consciousness and the lure of the Divine Light, although they do so in their own metaphors and images. In their own way they have learned how to enter alpha as they pray or worship. They learn how to become enlightened.

Yes, the processes of enlightenment can be learned by anyone, not just popes and bishops, gurus and lamas. Even an Aethiest can understand his/her own ability to create something out of nothing, just as he/she was created. The process doesn't care; it holds no prejudice. It will work for you whether you realize it or not. It never stops working (much to the distress of those who cannot figure out why they can never get enough of what they don't want!!!).

It just takes a hell of a lot of hard work and attention, something few of us have time or patience for anymore. In our age of high technology and accelerated progress, we often lose sight of the thoughts and beliefs that shape our perception, and thus, our manifest reality. We go through the motions, all the way up until our very last breath, when we look back and realize that we did not live the life we had truly wanted. And all because we were not paying attention to the foundations we were building with our dominant thoughts and actions. Maybe we Nevillized the wrong things, putting the power of feelings and emotions behind thoughts of anger, poverty, distress, disease, and unhappiness, when those same energies could have been the catalyst to a better, happier, and more fulfilled life.

Many Mansions, Many Roads

Controlling Our Lives Through Intention

Focus. Awareness. Attention. Intention. Feeling. In a world filled with distraction after distraction, just saying a few affirmations or thinking a few positive thoughts here and there won't bring us the creation we long to see as our personal, and global, reality. Imagine a world filled with people who are not sure of who they are, why they are here, and even where they are going, and you have a world filled with directionless thoughts and powerless intentions that never gel or formulate into anything of value. No wonder so many people are depressed, anxious, and ill.

But we all have the ability to change this, and to take control of our roles as both a creation of something grander than ourselves, and as creators ourselves, able to use the same processes and powers that we see on a more cosmic scale to bring the imagined world into fixed, physical form. Why not imagine, then, the best? If one person can do it, then anyone can do it. If one person can create a life of abundance, love, and meaning, then anyone can, because the process by which one creates that life is the same for each and every one of us.

The three aspects, of the Father as the Divine Creator, the Son as earthbound human, and the Holy Spirit as the Way/Process/Activating Agent exist for every human being no matter what race, color, creed, or religion. We are all living Trinities, Living Buddhas, Christs, shamans, sorcerers, and mythical heroes who venture forth from the common everyday reality into the supernatural realm in search of the Holy Grail. The Trinity is more than just a religious term based upon a grander metaphysical truth of our own, and God's, threefold nature. It is literally the Holy Grail itself, the key that unlocks the doorway to our own personal power to change and shape the outcomes of our lives.

This common spiritual ground, however, is not exclusive to the Trinity, for all great religious symbols have their origin in a common experience of humanity. Perhaps by closely examining the Trinity, and comparing and contrasting it among the religions and cultures mentioned here, we can spark interest in doing the same examination of other great religious archetypes and symbols. The virgin birth, for example, is not at all exclusive to Christianity. Virgin Birth stories appear throughout most religious systems and mythological traditions to describe the impending divinity of a common mortal. Buddha was the result of just such a virgin birth, a "signpost" of sorts that suggests his exalted state to come. Other powerful symbols not relegated to any one religion occur in the life/death/rebirth stories of ancient Greek, Norse, and Roman mythologies, and the Golden Bough tales of pagan traditions.

The cross itself is rampant with symbolic history dating far back beyond the birth of the Christian religion, and one can easily get lost for months reading about the commonalties of creation myths and stories. Then there are the hero tales, the legends of great men and women with supernatural, almost Messianic abilities. Some examples of this are Hermes (who, early Christians may have used as a model of the mythic Christ), Christ, Buddha, Krishna, and their mythological counterparts, as well as the legendary Knights of the Round Table and King Arthur himself (whom many scholars suggest is a rewriting of the Christ myth!). Other powerful archetypes that we could examine and cross-reference are those of the devil/trickster, the concept of heaven and hell, and the resurrection of Christ (which so closely parallels the nature/resurrection stories of ancient mythology and pre-Christian pagan traditions).

Collective Archetypes and the Trinity

Our world is alive with archetypes of the collective unconscious—symbols we are aware of on a surface level, but often know little about on a much deeper level. And yet it is this deeper level that truly affects our existence and growth. To live amid symbols and archetypes, and yet not know how to use them in our everyday life, is to live in a state of ignorance to the richness that lies just beyond the veil. Should we collectively pierce that veil, we would behold a common vision. Until then, understanding and truth will continue to be limited only to those who have eyes to see and ears to hear.

Perhaps this embracing of the commonalties of religions will bring about an end to what H.P. Blavatsky referred to as the "Age of

Churchianity," and hopefully usher in the "Age of the Holy Spirit," where each individual will discover for himself/herself the nature of the Divine within, and how best to express it.

After all, we are now leaving the confusing, watery realm of Pisces and entering the Age of Aquarius—the Age of Spiritual Enlightenment. There certainly couldn't be a better time to figure out what the wise sages of old have been trying to tell us all along.

The very act of co-creation from our intention is at our fingertips, as proven by exciting new discoveries in quantum physics. God said, "Let there be light" and there was light, and that Law of Creation applies to us as individuations of God. We, too, can be, say, and manifest. It is both exhilarating and heartening to know that these core metaphysical truths may someday be so widely embraced and understood that there will be no place in the world for intolerance, prejudice, or religious holy wars. Once we begin to celebrate the common spiritual ground we all stand upon, we can then appreciate the diverse beauty in which that common ground is tilled and sown, all destined to reap the same wonderful harvest.

That there indeed is one truth, that *The Trinity Secret* perfectly embodies that truth, and that knowing and understanding that truth will set us free and transform the collective consciousness of humanity.

God.	Said.	Light.
I.	Am.	That.
Creator.	Created.	Creation.

That, in three simple words, is the secret. Amen.

The Trinity Secret

Appendix: Some Famous Threes

Just a few famous threes:

- ❧ Body, mind spirit.
- ❧ Id, Ego, Superego.
- ❧ Explicate, implicate, superimplicate.
- ❧ Unconscious, conscious, superconscious.
- ❧ Father, Son, Holy Spirit.
- ❧ Brahma, Vishnu, Shiva.
- ❧ Keter, Yesh, Binah.

- Earth, sea, sky.
- Underworld, Middle World, Upper World.
- Earth, hell, heaven.
- Maiden, Mother, Crone.
- Atum, Cosmos, Man.
- Buddha, Dharma, Sangha.
- Birth, life, death.
- Beginning, middle, end.
- Te, Tao, Chi.
- Emanation Body, Beatific Body, Truth Body.
- Lucidity, passion, dark inertia.
- Esus, Toutatis, Touranis.
- Odin, Vili, Ve.
- Shen, Qi, Jing.
- Reptilian, mammalian, human brain.
- Three laws of motion (Newton).
- Three laws of planetary motion (Kepler).
- Three laws of thermodynamics.
- Triplet codon system of DNA.
- Three spatial dimensions.
- Three little pigs.
- Three bears.
- Three blind mice.
- Three little kittens.
- Three billy goats gruff.
- Three Fates.
- Three Graces.

- ❧ Three wise men (bearing three gifts!).
- ❧ Three wishes.
- ❧ Three tasks.
- ❧ Third time's the charm!
- ❧ Yesterday, today, tomorrow.

And a few just for fun:

- ❧ Manny, Moe, and Jack.
- ❧ Three Musketeers.
- ❧ Moe, Larry, and Curly. (Poor Shemp—he always got the shaft!)
- ❧ *The Three Amigos.*
- ❧ *Three Men and a Baby.*
- ❧ *Three Days of the Condor.*
- ❧ Winken, Blinken, and Nod.
- ❧ God, guts, and glory.
- ❧ Lock, stock, and barrel.
- ❧ Bed, Bath, and Beyond.

Some Famous Threes

Bibliography

Abraham, Ralph, Terrence McKenna, and Rupert Sheldrake. *The Evolutionary Mind: Conversations on Science, Imagination and Spirit*. Rhinebeck, N.Y.: Monkfish Publishing, 2005.

Baird, James, and Laurie Nadel. *Happiness Genes: Unlock the Positive Potential Hidden in Your DNA*. Franklin Lakes, N.J.: New Page Books, 2010.

Blatner, Adam, M.D. "The Relevance of the Concept of 'Archetype.'" Presented to the Department of Psychiatry, University of Louisville School of Medicine, Louisville, Ky., June 7, 1990.

Bohm, David. *Wholeness and the Implicate Order*. London: Routledge Classics, 2002.

Bohm, David, and F. David Peat. *Science, Order and Creativity*. London: Routledge Press, 2000.

Braden, Gregg. *Secrets of the Lost Mode of Prayer: The Hidden Power of Beauty, Blessing, Wisdom and Hurt*. Carlsbad, Calif.: Hay House, 2006.

Butin, Philip W. *The Trinity: Foundations of Christian Faith*. Louisville, Ky.: Geneva Press, 2001.

Campbell, Joseph. *Myths to Live By*. New York: Bantam Books, 1972.

Freke, Timothy, and Peter Gandy. *The Hermetica: The Lost Wisdom of the Pharaohs*. New York: Tarcher/Puttnam, 1997.

Gaffney, Mark H. *Gnostic Secrets of the Essenes*. Rochester, Vt.: Inner Traditions, 2004.

Haisch, Bernard. *The Purpose-Guided Universe: Believing in Einstein, Darwin, and God*. Franklin Lakes, N.J.: New Page Books, 2010.

Harner, Michael. *The Way of the Shaman*. New York: Bantam Books, 1980.

Jung, Carl. *Psychology and Religion: West and East—The Collected Works of C.G. Jung*. Princeton, N.J.: Princeton University Press, 1975.

———. *Synchronicity*. New York: Bollingen Foundation, 1960.

Luthi, Max. *The Fairy Tale as Art Form and Portrait of Man*. Indianapolis, Ind.: Indiana University Press, 1984.

Miller, Richard, and Iona Miller. *The Modern Alchemist: A Guide to Personal Transformation*. Grand Rapids, Mich.: Phanes Press, 1994.

Nabarz, Payam. *The Mysteries of Mithras: The Pagan Belief That Shaped the Christian World*. Rochester, Vt.: Inner Traditions, 2005.

Nichol, Lee. *The Essential David Bohm*. London: Routledge Press, 2002.

O'Collins, Gerald. *The Tripersonal God: Understanding and Interpreting the Trinity*. Mahwah, N.J.: Paulist Press, 1999.

Olson, Roger E., and Christopher A. Hall. *Guides to Theology: The Trinity*. Grand Rapids, Mich.: Wm. B. Eermans Publishing Co., 2002.

Sams, Gregory. *Son of God: Discovering the Self-Organizing Consciousness That Underlies Everything*. San Francisco, Calif.: Weiser Books, 2009.

Schaeffer, Joseph H. "Beliefs about Evolution, Mind, Nature, and Society: Excerpts from an Interview with Ervin Laszlo," *ZYGON* 23, no. 2 (June 1988).

Turner, Dr. John L. *Medicine, Miracles, & Manifestations*. Franklin Lakes, N.J.: New Page Books, 2009.

Vitale, Joe. *The Key: The Missing Secret For Attracting Anything You Want*. Hoboken, N.J.: John Wiley, 2007.

Webb, Hillary. *Exploring Shamanism*. Franklin Lakes, N.J.: New Page Books, 2003.

Index

About the Authors

Marie D. Jones

Marie D. Jones is the best-selling author of *PSIence: How New Discoveries in Quantum Physics and New Science May Explain the Existence of Paranormal Phenomena*. Marie is also author of *2013: End of Days or a New Beginning—Envisioning the World After the Events of 2012*, which features essays from some of today's leading thinkers and cutting-edge researchers. She co-authored with her father, geophysicist Dr. John Savino, *Supervolcano: The Catastrophic Event That Changed the Course of Human History*. She is also the author of *The Déjà Vu*

Enigma: A Journey Through the Anomalies of Mind, Memory, and Time; 11:11—The Time Prompt Phenomenon: The Meaning Behind Mysterious Signs, Sequences, and Synchronicities; and *The Resonance Key: Exploring the Links Between Vibration, Consciousness, and the Zero Point Grid,* with Larry Flaxman, her partner in ParaExplorers.com. She worked as a field investigator for MUFON (Mutual UFO Network) in Los Angeles and San Diego in the 1980s and 1990s, and co-founded MUFON North County. She currently serves as director of special projects for ARPAST—The Arkansas Paranormal and Anomalous Studies Team.

Marie began her extensive writing career as a teenager writing movie and video reviews for a variety of national magazines, as well as short stories, including award-winning science fiction and speculative fiction for small press genre and literary magazines. She is now a widely published author with hundreds of credits to her name.

Her first non-fiction book, *Looking for God in All the Wrong Places,* was chosen as the "Best Spiritual/Religious Book of 2003" by the popular book review Website RebeccasReads.com, and the book made the "Top Ten of 2003" list at MyShelf.com. Marie has also co-authored more than three dozen inspirational books for Publications International/New Seasons, including *100 Most Fascinating People in the Bible, Life Changing Prayers,* and *God's Answers to Tough Questions,* and her essays, articles, and stories have appeared in *Chicken Soup for the Working Woman's Soul, Chicken Soup to Inspire a Woman, If Women Ruled the World, God Allows U-Turns, UFO Magazine, The Book of Thoth, Paranormal Magazine, Light Connection Magazine, Alternate Realities, Unity Magazine, Whole Life Times, Science of Mind Magazine,* and many others. She is also a popular book reviewer for such Websites as BookIdeas.com and CurledUp.com.

Her background also includes more than 15 years in the entertainment industry, as a promotions assistant for Warner Bros. Records, film production assistant, and script reader for a variety of film and cable TV companies. She has also been an optioned screenwriter, and has produced several nationally distributed direct-to-video projects, including an award-winning children's storybook video. She currently has several film and TV projects in development, including "19 Hz the Movie" with Bruce Lucas Films.

The Trinity Secret

In her capacity as an author and researcher, Marie has appeared at several major conferences, including CPAK and the Queen Mary Ghost Hunting Weekends. She has been interviewed on hundreds of radio talk shows, including *Coast To Coast with George Noory*, NPR, KPBS Radio, *Dreamland*, and *The Shirley MacLaine Show*, and has appeared on television, including the History Channel's *Nostradamus Effect*. She has been featured in dozens of newspapers, magazines, and online publications all over the world and is currently developing projects for film and television. She lives in San Marcos, California, with her son, Max. Her Websites are *www.mariedjones.com* and *www.paraexplorers.com*.

Larry Flaxman

Larry Flaxman is the best-selling author of *The Déjà vu Enigma: A Journey Through the Anomalies of Mind, Memory and Time; 11:11— The Time Prompt Phenomenon: The Meaning Behind Mysterious Signs, Sequences, and Synchronicities*; and *The Resonance Key: Exploring the Links Between Vibration, Consciousness, and the Zero Point Grid* with Marie D. Jones, his partner in ParaExplorers.com. Larry has been actively involved in paranormal research and hands-on field investigation for more than 12 years, and melds his technical, scientific, and investigative backgrounds together for no-nonsense, scientifically objective explanations regarding a variety of anomalous phenomena. He is the president and senior researcher of ARPAST—The Arkansas Paranormal and Anomalous Studies Team, which he founded in February 2007. Under his leadership, ARPAST has become one of the nation's largest and most active paranormal research organizations, with more than 150 members worldwide dedicated to conducting research into the paranormal using the most stringent scientific methodology. ARPAST is a proud member of the TAPS family (The Atlantic Paranormal Society) from the popular SyFy Channel television show *Ghost Hunters*. Larry supervises a staff of fully trained researchers and more than $250,000 worth of top-of-the-line equipment. Widely respected for his expertise on the proper use of equipment and techniques for conducting a solid investigation, Larry also serves as technical advisor to several paranormal research groups throughout the country.

About the Authors

Larry has appeared in numerous print interviews, including features in local and regional newspapers, magazines, and online publications such as *The Anomalist, Times Herald News, Jacksonville Patriot, ParaWeb, Current Affairs Herald, Unexplained Magazine,* and *The Pine Bluff Commercial.* He has been interviewed for several local and regional news television outlets, such as *Ozarks First,* as well as national cable television, appearing in an ongoing paranormal series on JustinTV, as well as on Discovery Channel's popular show *Ghost Lab,* and he has been interviewed on hundreds of radio programs, including *Coast to Coast with George Noory, X-Zone, Ghostly Talk, Eerie Radio, Crossroads Paranormal, Binall of America,* and *Haunted Voices.* He currently has a feature film in development titled "19 Hz the Movie" with Bruce Lucas Films.

He is also co-creator (with Marie D. Jones) of ParaExplorers.com, devoted to the exploration of ancient and modern unknown mysteries, and is developing a line of related books and products. In addition, Larry is co-creator of the popular new ParaTracker software program for documenting data from paranormal investigations. His own ARPAST online research database system, SOCIUS, is considered one of the most comprehensive in the field. His enthusiasm for education and training in the paranormal field has also garnered many requests for special events and seminars, including popular charity investigations at haunted locations across the South, lectures on paranormal awareness for regional libraries, and appearances at major conferences.

Larry also currently works in law enforcement/information technology. He is married and lives in Little Rock, Arkansas. His Websites are *www.arpast.org,* and *www.paraexplorers.com.*